D1636329

Glory To God In The Highest
Ministries
PO Box 4677
Harrisburg, PA 17111

Glory to God in the Highest

*Visions and Divine Order
from the Lord*

Dereick P. Smith

McDougal Publishing is a ministry of The McDougal Foundation, Inc., a Maryland nonprofit corporation dedicated to the spreading of the Gospel of Jesus Christ to as many people as possible in the shortest time possible.

Published by:

McDougal Publishing
PO Box 3595
Hagerstown, MD 21742-3595

.www.mcdougalpublishing.com

ISBN 1-58158-083-5

Printed in the United States of America
For Worldwide Distribution.

DEDICATION

To my wife Edna: Next to the Lord, you are my dearest friend and greatest love. I love you! Thank you for having a great part in introducing me to a great man, Jesus Christ, and encouraging me to write this book and praying.

To my children, Dereick, Joe and Tammy: I love you all with the love of Christ, and I am proud to be your father.

ACKNOWLEDGMENTS

My deepest appreciation goes to...

Pastor Gordon K. Chirillo — thank you for your divine word from God.

Ellie Rivera — thank you for speaking a true word from God and for your prayers

Jennifer Lane — thank you for your prayers.

Maudessa Paskins — thank you for loaning me your typing skills on this project and for your prayers.

Pastor Phillip Cappuccio — thank you for your encouragement and for your prayers

Pastor Bob Smith — thank you for your encouragement and for your prayers.

CONTENTS

Prayer from the Pastor

Dear Lord, Please help me with this book. I can't do it alone. I need Your help. Anoint me Lord. Anoint me afresh, and speak what You want me to speak. Anoint me afresh to speak a true word, a spoken word, in this book.

Lord, help me perform the mission You have given me for this book. Even if it touches only one soul, or if only one person is saved, healed and delivered; even if one person doesn't commit suicide, if just one person sees who You are by reading these pages, then I will have accomplished the task You gave to me.

Lord, no matter what the cost or price to publish this book. No matter if I don't sell one copy, but have to give all of them away, if it saves just one life, then all the money spent to make this book has been well spent. That's the way I look at it—that's the way I have to look at it.

Writing all of this down and getting it into print is not about me looking good. It's not about me looking important, and it's not about me making any money. It's about reaching souls out here in this world. For I know Jesus wants everyone to go to Heaven. I know that not everyone is going to make it, but if I can be a part, even the tip of a needle, to help get a soul in the Kingdom, then I'll do my part.

I can't look at yesterday or tomorrow. I can only look at now, at what's happening now. What can I do for You, Lord? What can I do for You, my Lord? I want to help You grow Your Kingdom. I want to help You receive the glory. I want to be a vessel to help Your people. I know that this won't be easy; Your people are not easy. They are a stiff-necked and rebellious generation. After experiencing them, I can imagine what Moses went through. Moses had millions that he had to deal with. What an awesome challenge it is. What an awesome responsibility to serve the great I AM. Strengthen me for the task, O Lord.

Amen

Chapter One

In the Beginning

I first met my wife, Edna, in 1963. At the time, I was about fifteen years old, and I worked at my dad's gas station. To hear my wife tell it, the Lord told her that I would be her husband one day. Well, almost three years later, we married and fulfilled God's prophetic word to Edna. We married on October 16, 1965, both of us still very young. I was seventeen and Edna had just turned fifteen. It wasn't long after that we started our family. Over the years, we would be blessed with four children, one of which would pass on to glory at a young age.

In our early years, when the children were small, our marriage hit some rough times as nearly every marriage does. We had some differences, and those trials caused us to separate for a season.

At the time, 1968, the draft was in effect, drawing large numbers of young men into military service. Because I was reclassified as 1-A, I received a draft notice. I went to the army recruiter for information on how to change my classification. I had always wanted to be a paratrooper. To get into an airborne division, you had to be classified as RA, regular army, so I went back in a couple of days, after the change went through, and volunteered for the draft. This was December and it was the heart of winter.

After the New Year's break, I was sent to Fort Dix, New Jersey, for basic training. I found out then that the weather doesn't stop the army. We went to training with sheets of ice on the ground, in the snow, in the rain, and in every other type of weather.

We went through bayonet training with our M-14 rifles, and most of the NCOs were Vietnam vets. I was going through the obstacle course one day when the senior NCO heard me call my M-14 "a gun." He had me stand at attention and chewed me out to teach me that my M-14 was not "a gun"; it was a weapon. Then I had to run the obstacle course while holding my weapon over my head.

After nine weeks of training at Fort Dix, I was sent to Fort Gordon, Georgia, for advanced individual training, or AIT for short. I figured this training would be a breeze after basic training. I figured wrong. As soon as we got off the bus into formation, the cadre was shaking us down. We had to take everything out of our duffel bags right there in line.

At Fort Gordon, if the instructors knew you were headed for jump school they worked you harder and the training was mentally and physically tougher.

Everything was geared for airborne training. We ran every morning calling cadence as we went. We even had a C-119 aircraft sitting in the field next to our unit.

Everyone in our company was a volunteer for jump school at this point. After jump school, every man was headed for either a special forces unit or an airborne unit.

At this point, I knew that joining the military was far more than I had bargained for. I'd had no idea what I was getting into when I reported. They work you over in the military. It's completely true that only the strong survive. The weak fall by the wayside. By being so hard on us, they were able to weed out the weak men. They wanted only the strong ones. As I went through training, I told myself, "I will never come back here again." If I never saw Fort Gordon again after leaving there, it was fine with me.

We finally got through the ten weeks of AIT and graduation day came. The field officer read off the orders where each man was going from there. All the men who were dropped from the airborne or who canceled out of jump school were being sent to Vietnam. The rest of us were headed for jump school.

Chapter Two

Jump School

At jump school, we began both physical and mental training to get our bodies physically fit and our minds sharper so we could pay attention. The first week was ground week. The second was tower week. After that, we went into jump week.

The first aircraft I would be jumping from was a C-119, which was a prop aircraft. My mind was zeroed in on the jump ahead of me from the time we "chuted up" until the time the six-minute warning came. I had so much fear inside me that I prayed to God for all of this to work out, for a safe exit and a parachute-landing fall. Praying wasn't something I normally did a lot of, and God wasn't someone I knew very well, although I did believe in Him.

My mind went into gear and I just thought of what we were trained to do. Each step played through my mind. First, shuffle to the door, make a vigorous exit in tight body position, keep both hands on the reserve, count to four-one-thousand. Then fill the shock of the chute opening, check parachute, watch

for obstacles, check the drift you are going in, pull the right slip, relax in the harness, keep feet and knees together, prepare to land. After I prayed, all the steps stuck in my mind. I took my position at the door and away I went, following each step. Everything followed through perfectly. After I landed, I thanked God for this safe jump. I would take three more jumps from a C-119. My fifth jump was from a C-141 four engine jet aircraft.

The first time I ever had a chute malfunction was during a jump from the C-141. The C-141 is a jet aircraft. We were trained to make vigorous exits out of prop aircraft, but when it came time for us to jump out of the C-141 jet aircraft my mind was not on my exit. When I first saw this jet I had a big lump in my throat and I thought, "Oh my God! I'm jumping out of this big aircraft that looks like a spaceship." I asked myself, "What are you doing here, you fool! You've got to jump out of that jet."

It was so huge. Those models then held 120 paratroopers. We loaded the aircraft, the ramp lifted upward, and the doors went shut. The C-141 started taxiing towards the runway. The jet engine started to get louder, and before we knew it, we were rolling down the runway. The aircraft lifted off and we were airborne. When the aircraft lifted, it was just so awesome. I began thinking about the excitement of jumping from this plane. It was a different kind of plane, so the jump would be different.

When the aircraft leveled off, we got the twenty-minute warning (in a prop aircraft, it's a six-minute warning). When the twenty minutes came and went, we began to go through our jump commands and preparations: stand up, hook up, shuffle to the door, and stand by for the commands.

At this point, I was talking to God, and then praying again for a safe exit. One thing I can say for the C-141 is that this aircraft was a smooth ride. In the C-119, I would have sworn that the rivets were vibrating out of it. Today I don't know how that aircraft made it off the ground.

I knew it would not be long before I would be going out the door. Here I was asking God for help again. I prayed, but still felt my nerves were in a wreck. The door was open and the wind deflector went out. The wind deflector is like a small door. After the aircraft loadmaster opens the side doors of the aircraft, he hits a switch and a small door with small holes in it swings out where the door was. This door is a wind buffer, so that when the paratroopers go to exit the aircraft they don't get all the wind blowing on them at one time.

The jet aircraft can only slow down to a certain speed. I heard the wind deflector go out and lock into position. I could really hear the wind going through those holes; it was a loud rushing noise of air. The green light came on and one by one we began to go out of the C-141. We were taught to bunny hop out because of the jet engines.

When it came time to jump, instead of making a bunny hop, I made a vigorous exit like I would have from a prop aircraft. I must have made the best vigorous exit they ever saw because when I hit that jet stream, I was really moving. I didn't have to wait for an opening shock from my parachute opening. It was open in a fraction of a second. My harness felt like it was going right through me.

When I jumped, I had hit the jet stream from one of the jet engines. The engine just swooped me up. It picked me up and would have thrust me even more so if I hadn't hit that jet stream. I could smell the aircraft fuel and the smoke that was on me and when my chute opened I saw it was smoking. I looked around, but I didn't see myself falling any quicker than anyone else.

In a jump exercise, the black hat instructors on the ground below have bullhorns and when they see a paratrooper having a malfunction, they holler on the bullhorn, "Pull your reserve." Well, the black hats were hollering at me. They kept yelling, "Pull your reserve! Pull your reserve!" And several paratroopers were pulling their reserves because there was a high traffic up there. I didn't pull my reserve and when I hit the ground one of the black hat instructors came running over to me. He said, "You dummy, why did you jump out?"

I looked at my chute and it was still smoking. I looked at the black hat like a dummy and said, "I'm the fool for being here." I thanked the good Lord again for this jump. He picked me up off the ground and dragged me back to the parachute and pointed out that the chute was still smoking. It had all these little holes in it the size of nickels, quarters, fifty-cent pieces and some as big as baseballs. I paid dearly for that jump. Everyone in the unit harassed me and they stayed on me about it. From that time on I never made a vigorous exit from a jet aircraft.

There would be another time when I was nearly killed or injured in a jump. It happened after jump school when I had moved on to a regular unit. We were preparing to deploy to another part of the country for a jump.

We were going to be jumping into an unknown location. This time I had a bad feeling about jumping. It felt like something wasn't right—in fact, something definitely felt wrong, so I started praying, "Oh God, help me, help us all."

Once we were prepared and were over the target location, I jumped out of the aircraft. When I did, I looked up and saw a "Mae West." A Mae West occurs when one or two of your suspension lines wrap around your chute and it looks like you have two parachutes. In this situation, you're trained to go back into a tight body position and pull the cord for your reserve chute. I remained calm, cool and collected about it, so I went back into a tight body position and pulled my reserve.

Once I fed my reserve out, I thought I was all right. Until I looked up again, that is. Suddenly I saw my reserve chute wrapping around my suspension lines and coming down to the top of my harness. When it slid down on top of me, I could only see through a space under my armpit that I was falling very fast. I cried out, "Help me, God," and by the time I got the words out I hit the ground. I hit the ground hard-and-fast. There was a parachute rigger (that's a soldier who packs the parachute) on the drop zone when I hit. He came running over and tried to awaken me because I was unconscious. He pulled the ammo nitrate from his first aid pouch, broke the tablet, and placed it under my nose. He had to use two of them, and finally I came to.

When my eyes opened all I could see was a beautiful blue above me. It was the sky, and I had no idea where I was. I thought I was dead or somewhere else. When I finally got up, the rigger pointed out the imprint my body made on the ground because I had hit so hard. He looked at me in amazement and said, "The way you hit the ground and bounced up I thought every bone in your body had to have broken and that you were dead." I know now that it was only through the grace of God that I survived. The Lord saved me.

There would be one more near tragedy during a jump. Some time passed after the last incident and then we went on another mission. This mission was a night drop. We flew into a location on a small drop zone or landing zone, which is also called an LZ. I usually try to be the first or the last man to exit the aircraft, especially if it was a mass jump. I never liked to get in the middle of the line to jump out because of the traffic in the air. There was always a chance of drifting into someone else's chute, or having a mid-air collision, or walking on someone's chute. If these things happen, you run into problems.

On this particular mission, I was the last one to jump. I got up to the door and the jump master booted me right in the rear end. I went flying out the door headfirst and tumbled in a circle. When my parachute opened, I was hanging upside down. My head was where my feet should have been, and my feet were where my head should have been. My right leg wrapped into the suspension lines of the parachute. My body weight pulled down on my legs and my parachute pulled up. The chute just kept pulling and making the suspension lines tighter and tighter around my leg. I couldn't get my leg out. The more I pulled the tighter the suspension lines got until they were cutting into my leg.

Before going on a mission, we always had a jump briefing. We were told what the knots were on the drop zone, where our assembly area was, which way we would drift, etc. This particular time I was the last man out, so I knew I was at the end of the drop zone or LZ. At the end of the LZ there was woods, and a distance from the woods there was a river. I started thinking about not being able to get turned around to land feet first because I was upside down. I thought if I landed on the LZ, I was going to hit headfirst and possibly break my neck. If I landed in the trees, I would be headfirst and still break my neck. If I bypassed the LZ and the woods, I would end up in the river with my leg wrapped up in the suspension lines. I knew if I couldn't get out I would hit the river headfirst and the current pulling on the chute would drown me in the river. When silk gets wet, it is heavy.

I continued trying, but I couldn't get my leg out of the suspension lines. Even if I would hit the quick release on the harness to release the chute from my body, my leg would still be tangled in the suspension lines and I would drown. It didn't look too good. I knew I would soon be coming up to the LZ, and I thought, "I can pray." So I prayed, "God help me. Help me with this God," and about that time, my leg seemed to melt through the suspension lines. My feet came down to where my head was and my head to where my feet were. No sooner had my body flipped around to where it should have been than I hit the ground, landing on my feet. When I hit the ground, I didn't even have to make a parachute-landing fall. I hit so softly, like a feather, that I just stood there, and said, "Thank You, God. Thank You, because I know that this is another miracle for me."

In a paratrooper unit, any jump when you can get up and walk away is a good jump. It doesn't matter how hard you hit the ground, whether it's on your feet or if you have to fall and roll, or whatever else might happen, as long as you can get up and walk away, it's still a good jump.

For many years after those jumps, I wanted to terminate my enlistment, but I never had the heart to terminate from jump status. Ever since I was a child, I had wanted to be a paratrooper because of an uncle who had been a paratrooper in the special forces. I had always looked up to him.

Being a paratrooper like my uncle was a dream come true. I knew God had blessed me with His divine opportunity to be one, so I kept doing it for twenty-two years. And with every jump, I felt in my heart that God was working on me. God was making and molding me and shaping me into what He wanted me to be, not what I wanted to be. It was a progression that lasted twenty-two years of my life.

I didn't get to know the Lord Jesus as my Savior

until the latter part of my tour in the military. It was about the last, perhaps, eight to ten years of my life in the military when this happened. When I received Jesus as Lord and Savior, the Lord started revealing something in my life. Gifts began to come forth from the innermost part of my belly coming up out of me like rivers of flowing water. I had no idea what I had in there until the power of the Lord started showing up and coming forth.

As time went on, I realized it was my faith that had brought forth the spoken word. Faith is something so great and so important that the Bible mentions it over 300 times. The first reference to having faith in God is found in the story about Abraham. The Scripture says that Abraham *"believed in the LORD, and He counted it to him for righteousness"* (Genesis 15:6). This particular step of faith is so significant that the above statement is repeated three times in the New Testament in Romans, Galatians, and James.

The power of faith rests in the object of our faith. It's at the foundation of love. It is believing in the object that is loved. If we do not believe in a person, we cannot love her or him. The same is true in our spiritual journey. We must begin by believing that God exists, believing that He cares, and believing that His love is real. Glory Hallelujah! Hallelujah! Hallelujah!

Faith is also the key to getting our prayers answered. Hebrews 11 lists the Old Testament heroes of faith. Each one trusted God in a unique way. Their confidence in God's promises resulted in personal obedience to His will for their lives.

Chapter Three

A Turning Point

In spite of the difficulty of it, I made it through jump school. From there, I went to the 82nd airborne division for about a month, located at Fort Bragg in North Carolina. Later I received orders for temporary duty at West Point in New York to support and help train the officers going through the college.

While I was assigned to West Point, the Red Cross came and told me that there had been a death in my family. The company commander told me I would be going home. At the time, my wife and I were still separated, but right before this we had been writing letters back and forth discussing the possibility of reconciling. Now I would be going home to tragic circumstances.

No one would tell me what had happened or who had died. I went home to learn that our three-year-old son had drowned. I was devastated. My family was devastated. Yet, God will take the most horrible experiences of your life and make something good come from them. The loss of our son was a turning point in our marriage. His death drew Edna and I back together into a relationship much closer than we'd ever had before. I told her that as soon as I completed my tour at West Point we would go back to Fort Bragg and find a place for her and the children to live. Time would eventually see my wife and I grow so close together that it would completely change our lives.

After bringing my family to Fort Bragg and getting them settled, I went on various missions around the world. On most of these missions, in different locations, my unit would jump. It was during these missions that I really learned how to pray for the first time. I had always prayed—I had always believed in God, but I had never had a close relationship with Jesus Christ then. My wife did, but I didn't. It was in these times of risk, when my life was on the line with every jump, that I would pray heartfelt prayers drawing me closer to this God I believed in but didn't really know. Every jump took faith that He would see me safely to the ground. In a way, my paratrooper missions served as training for a future walk with the Lord. I learned that duty requires unquestioning obedience. I learned how to risk and believe. I learned how to pray and trust. Back then, I prayed for every jump...I still do.

Chapter Four

FINDING THE LORD IN PANAMA

In 1983, I was stationed in the Republic of Panama in Latin America as a senior NCO. My family was with me as well. Our daughter, Tammy, went to church with a friend one day. When she came home, she told Edna and I how much she enjoyed church. My wife was so impressed that she went the next Sunday.

The church they attended was an Assembly of God church that was housed in the old courthouse on the hill in Panama City. When she came home, she told me how much she had enjoyed this church. It sounded great the way she and Tammy described it and all that week Edna kept asking me to go with them the next Sunday.

When Sunday came I didn't go, but my two sons Dereick and Joe went with my wife and Tammy. Instead of going to church with them, I stayed at home and drank beer. I had been drinking since I was fourteen years old. During this tour in Panama over the previous seven months, I had been drinking even more than normal: two six packs and half a bottle of Seagram's a night. On weekends, I drank even more than that. Edna had already told me that if the drinking continued, she would take the children and go back to the states and it would be over between us.

When my family came home from church, I could see they were in unusually high spirits in the natural sense. Myself, I was high, but not naturally. My high was self-induced. Edna told me all I had to do was repent, have faith, and give everything over to Jesus. I thought about this all week, even at work.

At first, I didn't want to have anything to do with church or Jesus. I was busy performing my military duties and that was all I was concerned about. My wife continued going to this church for about three weeks. After the third Sunday, she came home and told me that this pastor looked identical to Kenny Rogers. She knew how much I liked Kenny Rogers and his music. I listened to it a lot, so my curiosity was now aroused.

The following Sunday I got up and was moving around the house when she asked me, "Well, where are you going today?"

I said, "I'm going to go to church and check out this man who looks like Kenny Rogers."

We arrived at the church on the hill and had to walk up a lot of steps. To me, it seemed there were more steps than I had imagined. It was a long way up. I made it to the top, but didn't want to go inside, but then I saw the pastor for the first time. He definitely looked like Kenny Rogers. In fact, I thought it really was Kenny at first, which is how much the pastor looked like him. The Lord used this to get my attention. The pastor greeted us, shook my hand, and gave me a hug.

When we went into the service and sat down, they were already in the midst of church services. The congregation stood up to pray, and someone started speaking in a strange language. I asked Edna what he was saying. She said she didn't know. I asked her what language he was, and she said it was called "speaking in tongues." Then the first man stopped speaking and someone else began to speak in English. I asked Edna what this man was talking about in English. She said he was interpreting what the first man had said in tongues. I was so confused, but then I remembered that this was a Pentecostal church.

As the service went on, the pastor had a prayer line and the people were lined up. He anointed their heads with oil and started praying for the individuals. Some of the people's knees went out from under them. They fell backward onto the floor and seemed to be out cold. I asked Edna what was happening to them, and she explained they had been "slain in the Spirit." I just could not comprehend all of this.

I had an urge to go to the altar, but I didn't want

to go up there in front of everyone because of my pride. My airborne paratrooper pride was very strong, and I didn't want to go up there. The service went on and they had an altar call. I saw Tammy, our six-year-old daughter, go up and kneel down at the altar.

I poked my wife and said, "Do you see our baby?"

My wife said, "Yes, honey."

I had no idea why she went up there, but I felt sympathy for her being up there by herself. I figured that maybe I would help her if I went up beside her. Little did I know that she was up there praying for me.

At the altar, the pastor asked me if I would like to receive the Lord Jesus Christ into my heart. I said, "Yes, I would." We prayed together, and after I received the Lord, he asked me if I wanted to receive the baptism in the Holy Spirit. I didn't have much understanding about that, but I was at the point of my life that I was ready to receive whatever God had for me. I knew my life needed to change.

The pastor talked to me and after that was over I stood up and he looked at me, and I saw something in that man's eyes that I had never seen before in my whole life. I saw the love of God in his eyes. His eyes just glowed with a pure light, and they seemed to just shine. I drew closer to him, and he looked at me and said, "Dereick, from this time forward, you will never be the same. All those old friends that you had are gone, and new ones are coming in. Your whole life has turned around for the good. You'll never be the same."

What he spoke that day was a true prophetic word, because ever since he spoke those words over me my whole life was never the same.

When we got home Edna showed me in the Bible everything that we had experienced in church that day. It was all right there in the Bible in black and white. I took that Bible, a King James Version, in my hand and could not put it down. I had a hard time understanding some of the scriptures though because of the old English language in it. Later, Edna would buy me an Amplified Bible and a Good News Bible. Then I would start to understand God's Word better. But then, I was thumbing through the King James. When I came to the book of Revelation, I was so interested that I had to read the whole book.

As I read God's Word, the desire to change began to grow in my heart. I started praying, "Lord, if I am going to commit to following You, I want to do it right. I need delivered of cigarettes and alcohol and I can't do it myself. I need Your help with this."

The following Sunday, I went to church and went straight to the altar. I had reached the place where I didn't care if anybody was looking or what anyone thought. I believed the altar of prayer was where I would be closest to Jesus Christ. I needed help and I knew it. Alcohol was messing up my life and destroying my family. I desperately didn't want to lose my family. So I knelt down at the altar and asked the Lord to deliver me, and I believed in my heart that He would.

The following week, my wife took all the whiskey bottles in the cupboard and dumped them all out. The Lord told her to leave the beer in the refrigerator, to just leave it alone, but to dump out all that hard liquor. She dumped all whiskey. When I came home from work and found out, I felt only peace about it. It didn't bother me one bit. God had given me His peace. I continued to drink the beer for a while.

The following week or two I still went up to the altar. I went up there because I felt led, and because I felt closer to Jesus there. I was a babe in Christ at that point and didn't know that I could make an altar anywhere. It could have been at the bottom of the ocean, in another galaxy, or anywhere in the world.

At the altar, I got down on my knees again and I asked the Lord for the desire of my heart. "Lord," I said, "I would like to be the first sergeant of the combat support company that I'm in. It's the biggest company in the battalion. We have more vehicles, more men, and more heavy weapons for the infantry than any other battalion." Normally what I was requesting would not take place in the army because of partiality. But I asked to be the first sergeant of that company and I left it with God. He could decide whether or not to bring it to pass.

Time passed and about a month and a half later, I

received a phone call on a Friday evening at my quarters. It was the sergeant major of the battalion I was in. He said, "Sergeant Smith, I want to be the first one to congratulate you. You've made the E-8 list. I want to see you Monday morning. Come on up and we will talk about your future."

I said, "Okay, sergeant major."

On Sunday, I went up to the altar and I thanked the Lord. I knew it had come by His hand because there were other NCO's in that battalion with more seniority than I had. They didn't understand why I'd been promoted and there was some jealousy about it. But, I knew full well why it had happened, so I gave thanks.

[typesetter: insert photo of author in uniform with "US Army" lettering on it.]

When Monday morning came, I went up to battalion headquarters to see the sergeant major. He said to me, "Well, Sergeant Smith, what would you like to do?" He was referring to my choice of job due to my promotion. Normally that doesn't happen because your superiors tell you what to do.

Since the sergeant major asked me what I would like to do, I said, "I want to be the first sergeant of the combat support company I am in."

He looked at me strangely and said, "You know that doesn't normally happen in the army."

I asked him for permission to speak freely. He

agreed to that, so I replied, "There are five platoons in my company. I know the mission of each platoon and all of their weapons and how they're used, so I know when they're doing their jobs right and that is the first sergeant's responsibility."

He said, "I will go in and talk to the battalion commander." I waited. After he finished talking to the battalion commander, he came out and said, "Well, first sergeant, you go down there and take care of that company. I will have orders cut for you to be the first sergeant of that company."

That definitely blew me away. Little did I know what I was asking for. I had no idea what I was getting into. So, I went down and started running the company. This company was an elite battalion comprised of airborne paratroopers, special forces units, and ranger units. The position given to me was a great responsibility. Because of my faith, the Lord had blessed me with this responsibility and granted my prayer request. We had an elite battalion and we would have an awesome mission within that battalion. But even as the military assigned me a great responsibility, the Lord would also give me some awesome missions and great responsibilities as I performed the job He had given me within this company.

Chapter Five

A DIVINE MISSION FROM THE LORD

Soon after receiving my promotion to first sergeant, things started getting hot in Panama and Honduras for the US military there. We began to have special teams going on special duties to various countries within Latin America.

My unit was deployed to Honduras to help train the Hondurans because the Russians were sending tanks into Nicaragua. They were headed down toward the border of Nicaragua and Honduras. Our mission was to go train the Honduran army with a new weapon that we had given them.

When we got back, I had so much work to do that I was burning a lot of candlelight in the company. One night around 9:00 PM, I finished in the orderly room and went to the dayroom. Our dayroom was the largest in the battalion. We had two national match pool tables for the soldiers. They were still shooting pool when I went in.

I went over to the beer machine and got a can of Miller Lite. At the time, a can of beer was about fifty cents. I stood there drinking it while I watched some men play pool, and as I finished that can of beer I heard the Lord tell me, "Son, that's the last beer that you will drink—you are delivered."

I was stunned because I actually heard a voice speak those words into my head. I hadn't ever heard this voice before. There was no one around me, but I knew this was God. From that day forward I was delivered from alcohol. He delivered me right then and there, and to me that was a miracle.

The following week I got very sick. I was so sick that I couldn't walk. If I tried, I stumbled and fell. My whole equilibrium was off balance. My head hurt so badly that my wife took me to the hospital. The doctors examined me and gave me some shots of medication to relieve the pain. They relieved it a little bit, but not much. This went on for about a week to ten days. It was so bad that I couldn't work. I couldn't even go out of the house because I couldn't walk straight and both my ears were messed up. I couldn't hear out of them.

My head was hurting so badly one night that I cried out. I said, "God, I need healed. Man can't heal me. The medicine they have is not doing anything. I am not healed. I need your help, Lord. I prayed one whole day. That night at 3:00 AM in the morning I was looking up at the ceiling. There were no lights on in the bedroom, but when I looked up I saw a word across the ceiling lit up like a neon sign. It read, "J-A-M-E-S 5." It was so bright that it hurt my eyes. I lay there and looked at it, thinking that I must be dreaming. I touched myself and I touched my face to make sure I was awake. I put my hands over my eyes and took them away again. Again, there was no doubt that I was awake. I just lay there and looked at it: James 5.

I woke my wife up then. You have to realize that I was still just a babe in Christ. I woke Edna and said, "Hon? Hon! Do you see that up there on the ceiling?"

She said, "Do I see what?"

"Do you see that?" I pointed at it.

"I don't see anything," she replied. "What do you see?"

I told her, "It's a word. It says, 'James 5.'"

She said, "Dereick, James is a book in the Bible. The Lord is talking to you. He wants you to get the Bible out and read it. Go read James chapter 5."

So I got the Bible out and went into another room, turned the light on, and started reading the whole chapter. When I got to James 5:13-14, the Lord illuminated those words in those verses as though a light was shining on them. This utterly blew me away. It was all I could do just to continue reading, but I did and this is what I read:

Is anyone among you suffering? Let him pray. Is anyone cheerful? Let him sing psalms. 14. Is

> *anyone among you sick? Let him call for the elders of the church, and let them pray over him, anointing him with oil in the name of the Lord. And the prayer of faith will save the sick, and the Lord will raise him up. And if he has committed sins, he will be forgiven.* James 5:13-15

After I read that passage, I went back to the bedroom and woke up my wife and read it to her. She asked me if I wanted to get a hold of Pastor Ship in the morning and I said yes.

When morning came, we called Pastor Ship and he told her he would meet with us. My wife took me down to the church on the hill in Panama City. We had to walk up a few steps, maybe twenty or thirty, and we walked inside to the pastor's office and sat down.

The pastor looked at me and just started talking to me. We must have sat there and talked for about an hour. I had no idea at the time what he was doing, because I was still just a babe in the Lord. Now I know that he was trying to determine the depths of my faith. He wanted to see if I truly believed in the Lord and had enough faith to believe in the Lord's healing power.

Finally, he said, "Dereick, if I take this anointing oil, and anoint and pray over you will you believe that the Lord will touch you and heal you?"

I looked at him and said, "Pastor, I have no choice, but to believe. Man cannot heal me. Medicine is not healing me. I believe the Lord will touch me and heal me."

He said, "Okay then," and he took that anointing oil, poured it over my head, and laid hands on me and prayed for me. Afterward, he said, "When you leave here, you keep praying like this: 'No weapon formed against me will prosper' and 'the stripes of Jesus has healed me.'" The pastor was quoting from the Bible these passages of scripture:

No weapon formed against you shall prosper, And every tongue which rises against you in judgment You shall condemn. This is the heritage of the servants of the Lord, And their righteousness is from Me," Says the Lord.

Isaiah 54:17

But He was wounded for our transgressions, He was bruised for our iniquities; The chastisement for our peace was upon Him, And by His stripes we are healed.

Isaiah 53:5

…who Himself bore our sins in His own body on the tree, that we, having died to sins, might live for righteousness; by whose stripes you were healed.

1 Peter 2:24

The pastor asked me if I could continue to quote

these verses and believe on them. I told him I would do so. My wife and I got up then and thanked him as we left his office.

Halfway down that long set of stairs we had climbed coming in, I suddenly felt a release of something in my body. I stopped right where I was and said to Edna, "Hold it!" She had her arms around me for support and together we just stood there as I felt the Lord touch me. I can't begin to describe the sensation. It seemed as though a newness was filling me up inside, and I knew at that moment that I was healed.

The Lord healed me that day coming down the steps from that old church that used to be a courthouse. That was in 1983. My wife and I have walked through various troubles in our lives since then, but each time we face something difficult, the Lord reminds me of the time He showed me James 5 lit up on the ceiling of my bedroom. Even though the trial may not always have been an illness, the Lord reminds me of that time to build my faith for whatever I'm facing in the present. That miracle gives me the encouragement and faith to go onward. I stop looking at the size of the trial, and suddenly remember the size of my God, and I know He can do anything, now and forever and ever.

James 5 is one of many scripture passages that remind me of what God has done for me. I know He can do the same for anyone if people would only give Him a chance, if they would only believe.... I believe if a person simply says, "I believe," then they are saved. If someone has enough faith to say, "I believe God has done this for me," and that person confesses his or her belief, then they are saved and born-again. God's Word tells us in John 3:15, *"that WHOEVER BELIEVES IN HIM should not perish but have eternal life,"* and it tells us in verse 16, *"For God so loved the world that He gave His only begotten Son, that WHOEVER BELIEVES IN HIM should not perish but have everlasting life"* (emphasis mine).

If simply believing in Jesus can provide us with the greatest miracle, salvation, then why should we doubt that it would provide healing?

As the days and weeks went on after God healed me, I went back to work performing my duties as a first sergeant back in garrison duty. Every chance I could, I would go home for lunch. There would usually be ten to fifteen women in our quarters praying. Their presence didn't bother me. I would just go into the kitchen, make myself a sandwich and eat. After eating, I would sit and listen to them pray. As they prayed, I felt so peaceful and relaxed. I knew that this was the peace of God. No one knew how much I really needed to hear the prayers.

One day as I sat listening, a little old woman suddenly came into the kitchen. I don't remember her name now, but she was a Spanish woman. She came over and put her arms around my shoulder and asked me, "Honey, can we pray for you? Do you need strength?"

I said, "Yes, I do." So I went into the room with the ladies and they put me in the center of their prayer circle and started praying for me. As they were praying, I kept feeling the peace of God. It began to fill me up, giving me strength. Finally, this peace became so strong and so tender that I began to weep like a baby. Soon I was weeping uncontrollably and the thought that came into my mind was "You're a paratrooper. You belong to an elite military force. You have no business crying like this."

I had to rebuke that thought, because the more I cried the more I felt a release and a cleansing in my soul and body. I felt refreshed and renewed. God filled me up with more of Him. I didn't understand this at the time, but He was moving on me and working in me to make me who He wanted me to be instead of who I had wanted to be. As the women prayed over me, I began to pray for myself, saying, "Lord Jesus, help me to be determined to live for You and to have a purpose in my heart for You. Let my life be about what You want, Lord, and not what I want."

For several weeks and months, I received a lot of prayer from the ladies and each time experience such peace that I would surrender myself over to Him again.

Soon, several missions started coming down from command. Several teams were going to be sent in different directions out of the country. For a couple of months, I was in Florida. When I returned, the company commander told me not to bother unpacking my bags because I was going to Puerto Rico.

In Puerto Rico, I was the senior NCO for the U.S. military's infantry sent to train their army on heavy weapons. At the time, I was the only senior NCO in the infantry unit who knew the tactics and technical information for some of the special weapons we were teaching them to use.

When I came back from that mission, I went right back to my duties as a first sergeant again, while supporting other units in other countries. Soon it all started taking a toll on me because I was putting in so many hours. It was wearing me down as well as the rest of my company.

The Lord, of course, knew this. He woke me up again one night at three o'clock in the morning, and said, "Dereick, I want you to take anointing oil and go anoint the company."

I thought, *here we go again. I must be dreaming.* I touched myself to make sure that I really was awake. As before, I woke up my wife, saying, "Honey, the Lord woke me up again."

Edna responded, "Did He say something?"

I told her that He had told me to take some anointing oil and go anoint the company. I said, "Honey, you're more experienced with spiritual things. You know about anointing with oil better than I do. How about if you do it and I'll tag along."

She declined. "The Lord told you to do it, so you had better do what He says." So I got up and dressed, and then I took the anointing oil and headed my vehicle down toward the barrack where my company was housed. On my way there, the enemy began to flood my mind with thoughts meant to dissuade me. *The soldiers have liberty now,* I thought. *They can go in and out all night long. What if someone sees me?* I could almost hear the questions and the sneers. *Look at the first sergeant He's sneaking around the company doing something. It looks like he has a little bottle of something. He's putting some of whatever that stuff is on the buildings and doors. I believe the first sergeant is flipping out.* Those kinds of thoughts filled my mind, and I had to wash them away with the blood of Jesus. I started praying. I began to pray some of the prayers the women had prayed over me in the kitchen.

Down at the barrack, I got out of the vehicle, took the oil out of my pocket and prayed over it. Then I walked around the whole building. I anointed the corners, the doors, and the windows, while sneaking around and peeking to see if anybody was watching me. I didn't see anyone watching me, so I walked inside the building to check in with the CQ (Charge of Quarters). This is the soldier who is in charge of the quarters of the company in the absence of the first sergeant and the company commander. If anything happens, the CQ notifies the first sergeant.

I walked in and the CQ said, "First sergeant, are you up and ready for a mission already?"

I said, "Yeah, serge, a divine mission." I walked to the orderly room and made a pot of coffee. I was just standing there waiting for the coffee to brew when the Lord spoke to me again. This time He told me to take the anointing oil and go anoint every door of every soldier's quarters in the barrack.

At that stage of my faith, I talked to the Lord the same way I talk to a person. That's just the way I was at the time, and I didn't know any better. I always called the Lord Buddy, so I said, "Buddy, You are a character. You want me to go anoint all of the rooms where the soldiers are quartered?"

I had a hard time accepting this particular mission because out of almost 200 soldiers in this company, there were always a few of them that were up all night. Some of them were partying, talking, playing cards, or they were doing something else because they would be off duty the next day.

The Lord didn't answer my question. He didn't need to. He knew I had heard Him and understood, I was just hesitant. I thought, *Why me Lord, why me? Why do I have to do this?* But I said, "Okay, Lord." I took that bottle of oil and marched onward with it.

On the first floor, I looked all round, listening for anyone who might be awake. I didn't hear anyone, so I started anointing the soldiers' doors. I walked by the latrine. Normally, there was always someone on the floor who was in the latrine, brushing his teeth or taking a shower or just using the toilet. Tonight there wasn't one soul in there. I anointed the entrance way to the latrine. I kept looking around, sneaking and peeking, hoping not to be seen. Nothing moved on that first floor.

On the second floor, I went to every room and anointed the doors and the latrine. Not one soldier was out of his room. Not one soldier was in the latrine. Not one soldier was walking down the hallways or corridors. On the third floor, it was the same. Not one soul stirred as I went about my mission. I had now anointed three floors and no one was stirring on any of them. I finished and went back down to the orderly room.

Back in my office, I walked in and the coffee was brewed. I could smell it. I was standing there getting ready to reach out my hand to grab the coffee pot with one hand and a coffee cup with the other, when all of a sudden a breeze blew over me.

It blew right on me and almost felt as though it went through me. No windows were open and it definitely hadn't come from the air conditioners.

I stopped moving my hands for the coffee and just stood there. Suddenly I smelled a fragrance that came from somewhere to my right. This fragrance passed in front of me and got stronger and stronger. Then it started getting a little weaker, as it passed by me.

It suddenly dawned on me that the breeze and the fragrance were evidences that the Lord was walking by me. I had never smelled a fragrance like that in my whole life. To this day I have never smelled a fragrance like it. When that breeze went by me like it did and the fragrance passed by me, I felt a release in my body. An energy came into me like a strong feeling of peace. I had never felt anything like it in my whole life. I knew it was the Lord who had walked by me. I knew there was no other explanation for what I had felt and smelled. I was awestruck that the Creator of the universe had taken the time to acknowledge my simple obedience to Him.

After that experience, I continued going to church every Sunday. Every opportunity that came to go to church, I was there, and I continued to carry and use the anointing oil.

There had been something about the use of anointing oil and it blessed me to see people be anointed with it. I took the use of the oil very seriously. In fact, I think people sometimes thought I took it too seriously. I had emptied some little perfume bottles of my wife's and filled them with frankincense and myrrh, and I carried them everywhere I went.

I always anointed myself wherever I went. Regardless of what I was doing, I would pray over the task and anoint myself because I believed it was the right thing to do.

The first time I went on a mission carrying a bottle of anointing oil in my jacket pocket, we were in the jungle and moving around. I bumped up against a tree or something and broke the bottle. All the oil ran down into the inside of my fatigue jacket pocket and left a big round circle of wetness that seeped through to the outside.

I felt lost without the anointing oil. It had become a part of me. When I went on missions, I was the type of person who always got involved with my people. We had the largest company, and in the company we had five platoons. I would take turns going out with different platoons on different missions. I'd even gone out with scout platoons when they went on patrols. I just liked being with the soldiers and talking to them, to really get to know them.

Well, something came up on this mission, and I forgot I had broken the bottle of oil. I was going to anoint myself and remembered I didn't have any oil. There was a dirt road beside the trail we were hiking. As I approached the dirt road, a private came down the road in an army jeep. I stepped out and waved to stop the jeep. The private saw me, saw that I was a first sergeant, and in respect for my rank, he stopped.

I began talking with him. As I did so, I thought of a way to get some oil. I asked the private if he always did his before operations checks whenever he drove a vehicle on a mission. He said yes, but that he didn't do a during operations check. It was standard operation to do a before, during, and after maintenance check on vehicles.

I told him to open the hood of the jeep. When he complied, I pulled out the dipstick. Just as there should have been, there was motor oil on the dip-stick. I figured oil was oil and the Lord would understand that this was all I had at the moment. I prayed over it and anointed myself with the oil from that jeep's engine. I did it because I believed that if I anointed myself with oil, any oil, that the Lord would answer my prayers. I believed.

People think you are crazy when you do stuff like I did that day, but that was where I was in my faith at that point in time. I was still young in the Lord and didn't know any better. It was my way of looking to the Lord for my protection and my provision. I believed it worked and to me that was all that counted. Today, I still believe God honored that time when I went out of my way to find oil in a jeep engine to anoint myself. I believe I was led of the Lord to do so, even though it made no common sense. But God's Word tells us that faith doesn't always make common sense from man's point of view. In the book of Proverbs, we read,

> *Trust in the Lord with all your heart, And lean not on your own understanding; In all your ways acknowledge Him, And He shall direct your paths.*
> Proverbs 3:5

I learned after that incident to start carrying little bottles of oil in each of my pockets. There were four pockets on my jungle fatigues and six pockets on my cargo pants. I carried oil in every pocket just to make sure that I would have oil with me when I needed it.

I *believed* God honored my prayers when I used the oil and that was where I was in my faith during that season of my life. Just like the worship song, "Sanctuary," which says, "Lord prepare me to be a sanctuary, pure and holy, tried and true. With thanksgiving, I'll be a living sanctuary for You."

In that season with the anointing oil, I even took it when I was in garrison. The Lord told me, "Dereick, take the oil and go anoint every vehicle in your unit." We had more vehicles than the whole battalion combined. So I took the oil to the motor pool where I anointed and prayed over every vehicle. *I believed.* I believed we would not lose one soldier in that unit—I believed that. Because the Lord told me to go anoint the vehicles, I knew He was watching over them. He had assigned me as His prayer warrior for the men under my care. I don't doubt that there were others who prayed for the men also, but even if God had only one prayer warrior in that unit to pray over those 200 soldiers, I believed He would honor those prayers.

I prayed for my unit all the time. I prayed for every one of those soldiers on a regular basis. One day in particular, I saw the evidence that my prayers were definitely effective.

We were deployed on a night mission, and our

company was broken up into smaller patrols. We were instructed to go and secure the Panama Canal because of a crisis. Although I didn't have to, I went with one of the patrols. That's how I was about my men. I didn't put them into any situation that I wasn't willing to face myself.

My patrol went into one area that was so thick and dense that it took forever just to go a short distance. That's how thick the jungle was. After a time, we came to a clearing. It was no more than a radius of 25 or 40 meters across. We sat at the edge of it, resting.

We were all sitting back to back with the radio in the middle. I was leaning back with my legs crossed, and I had the muzzle of my M-16 pointed across my legs away from me. As I sat there, I sensed something was out there moving, but I had no idea what it was. I got an uneasy feeling.

Suddenly to the right of the clearing, something came out of the jungle into the clearing. I could see it moving near the bushes. We had our night goggles with us, so I slowly put them on. When I looked over where I had seen the movement, I saw the biggest cat I had ever seen in my life. It started walking out into the clearing and then suddenly stopped and looked right at us. It must have picked up our scent, because it started heading in our direction.

I prayed silently, *Lord, take that big cat out of here.* The cat kept coming. It was walking in a low crouch like cats do when they are creeping up on their prey.

Slowly it came nearer. I reached down slowly to move the selector switch on my weapon to the fully automatic setting. I had a banana clip in there with about thirty rounds, and I prayed, *Lord, if this cat keeps coming closer, I'm going to have to shoot it, and I don't want to shoot your cat. But if it doesn't go away, I'll off load all thirty rounds into that cat.* I'm telling you it was a big cat! And, it was getting closer and closer.

With my right hand, I held my weapon in the cat's direction, and with my left hand, I slipped the night goggles off. I could see that the cat was no more than thirty away feet. From that distance, I could tell that it was a black panther. My heart was pounding so fast that I couldn't keep up with the beats. I thought, *oh, my God get this cat away from us.*

The cat stopped and seemed to be looking straight at me with those big green eyes. It took a few more steps. I got ready to squeeze the trigger of my weapon. The cat stopped and I was getting ready to squeeze the trigger when all of a sudden the cat turned around and began to walk away. It stopped for a brief instant to look back at me again, and then it turned and left. I said, "Thank you, Jesus. Glory hallelujah!" I was very relieved. Never in my whole life had I encountered such a big animal.

Two nights later we were on patrol in a different location when we heard a scream that sounded like a woman in agony. It was a loud scream that pierced right through my heart. We'd heard these types of screams before and knew it was the panther. A panther sounds just like a woman screaming in pain. When I heard it, I said, "Lord, You definitely have a disobedient cat. I thought You got rid of him." Apparently that cat was tracking us. Fortunately, thanks to prayer, we didn't have another close encounter like before. I figured the Lord must have made us smell so bad that the cat couldn't stand to be near us. That was fine with me!

Chapter Six

THE WORD OF THE LORD

While still stationed in Panama, my wife, Edna had a friend whose husband was in an artillery unit housed just up the street from my company. My wife and I went to visit them at home one evening. This was the first time I had ever met her.

As we were sitting at the table drinking a cup of coffee, this friend, Ellie kept looking over at me with eyes that seemed to see straight through me. She had the kind of stare that seemed capable of going right through your head and into your thoughts. Edna hadn't known her long and I didn't know her at all, but she somehow seemed to know everything about me. The whole encounter was blowing me away. That was the first time in my life that I had ever met a prophet.

Ellie had the gift of prophecy and with it, she had deep discernment and the gift of the word of knowledge. Ellie was the first person God used to tell me to write a book. This was around 1983. Ellie said, "You write a book, Dereick. God is with you, and it will be a best seller." I didn't think much of it at the time.

About a month later, I was sitting in the orderly room doing some paperwork. I sat back on the chair, and suddenly the Lord spoke to me. He said, "Dereick, what that prophetess told you—that was Me. I want you to write a book."

The presence of God hit me so hard, and felt so heavy that I just sat there and wept. I called my wife and told her what had happened.

Not long after that, the Lord woke me up in the middle of the night again. I checked my clock and sure enough, it was 3:00 AM. For some reason, He would always wake me up at 3:00 AM.

He told me to go open my closet and clean the closet out. I didn't understand. Clean what out of the closet? I just sat there on the bed and couldn't move. I started breaking out in a cold sweat and trembling. I couldn't even go to the closet.

My wife woke up. She saw the state I was in and asked me what was wrong. I told her what the Lord had said, but that I didn't understand, and she said, "You know, you probably have things in there the Lord wants you to get rid of."

I said, "Hon, that must be it, but I can't move or even go over near it."

She laid her hands on me and started praying in her prayer language. When she finished praying, I had the courage to go do it. I opened that closet and the Lord led me right to my army paperwork. I opened one particular folder and stored inside were all the school certificates that I had earned during my military career. For every school that you go through in the military, they give you a certificate of graduation. I had some certificates in there from when I went through army NCO academy.

Normally on these certificates, there are background pictures. This one certificate from the Third Army NCO Academy in Fort Bragg, North Carolina, was one of the hardest discipline schools I attended. On each corner of that certificate there was a dragon with flames shooting out of its mouth. The Lord told me to anoint it and lay it to the side, so I did just that.

Next I pulled out another certificate. This one I had earned when I went through JOTC, Jungle Operation Training Center. They had trained me to survive and overcome in the jungle. This certificate had king cobras on each side of the certificate. Those two snakes were facing one another with their mouths opened and their fangs showing, like they were ready to strike. My name was printed in big bold letters in the middle of it. The Lord told me to anoint that one also, so I anointed it and laid it aside with the first.

I went through other certificate and diplomas that had demonic pictures on them. One by one the Lord had me anoint them. When I had gone through the whole folder and had a pile of anointed paperwork, the Lord told me to burn them right then. That command was hard for me. These certificates represented the hardships, struggles, discipline and the pride I had put into my achievements in these military schools. I was proud of them.

I realized that if I was going to commit my life to serving the Lord, I needed to obey Him. I had to choose between my own pride and whether I wanted to please the Lord. I thought, *Lord, I'm serving You now. I have to do everything I can to do right and to please You. I know that isn't easy, but You can make it a smoother road for me. If this is what I have to do to draw closer relationship to You I will just have to do it.*

I took all of those diplomas and certificates outside and put a match to them. It's hard to explain, but the fire that burned them was not very bright. As they burned, there was a darkness to them. The fire was different, not like a normal, regular fire. When I burned them, it was like those certificates were alive the way they seemed to squirm and move as they burned. When it was finished, I wondered what the Lord would require of me next.

Time went on and the Lord continued the process of cleaning me up and making me what He wanted me to be for Him. He was taking the stinking pride out of my heart and putting it right where it belonged. Pride will get you nowhere. Pride will stop you from coming into a one-to-one friendship with God the Father. He wants to be a buddy, a friend that you never had before, but pride can prevent that fellowship. I had pride that I had to get rid of—pride from graduating jump school, pride from being in various elite units in the army. There was much pride in my heart and He knew that I had to get rid of all that pride because it was stopping me from coming closer to Him. Hallelujah! Hallelujah! Thank You, Jesus.

Not long after I burned my certificates, my wife began to spend a lot of time with her friend, Ellie. One evening when we were visiting Ellie at her house, we were talking and she suddenly began to give us a prophetic word. She told me, "Dereick, I see you in a black suit, and I see you preaching, and your preaching a word so awesome that it's getting the attention of the people. The people are grabbing a hold of it because it's a word they have never heard before. I see you doing this. I see you as a preacher." I thanked her for the word.

When her husband, Joe, came home from partying and having a good time, I talked to him a little bit before he went up to bed. Joe wasn't saved and the Lord told me to take a cup of coffee and go up and talk to him. I took the coffee up to him.

Joe was a supply sergeant in the army. He was really a jack-of-all-trades, and he had helped me out a lot with supplies. He could wheel and deal with the best of them and get you about anything you wanted. I asked Joe if he wanted a cup of coffee, and he replied, "Why not?" So, we started talking about things and eventually our conversation came around to the topic of the Lord.

I sensed the Spirit prompt me to ask Joe if he would like to know the Lord. Joe got a strange look on his face and said, "Yeah, I would." By this point he was pretty sober. We had been talking for a couple of hours before we got to this question, so he was definitely in his right mind.

I led Joe to the Lord right there and then. He was the first person the Lord used me to minister to — the very first one.

After that night, the Lord would start using me in different situations and different places to minister to different soldiers in the company. Even though I was being used of the Lord, I still had my own issues to overcome. I still had a problem in my life that needed to be resolved. I needed delivered from using swear words, or cussing, as we called it where I came from.

In spite of my growing relationship with the Lord, I still cussed a lot, especially when I got around the soldiers. I hardly cussed at all around my wife and children, but when I was around that bad-boy spirit in the unit I could swear with the best of them. I knew it was wrong, but I was powerless to stop on my own. Fortunately, when the Lord starts to clean you up, He doesn't leave any corner undone.

One day I was standing in front of the company building getting ready to walk around the corner to check out the soldiers' training. A private came around the corner and ran right into me. He got a wide-eyed look of astonishment on his face when he realized he had run right into his first sergeant.

I said, "Private, where do you think you're going in such a hurry?"

Before he could answer, I ordered him to get down and knock out ten airborne pushups. He dropped and started doing the pushups, but his chest wasn't touching the ground. To do airborne pushups, your chest has to touch the ground. I yelled at him to get his chest on the ground with each pushup, and I started cussing at him for emphasis. When he was all done and worn out, I pulled him up to his feet and called him a "yardbird." The word just came out of my mouth, surprising even me.

The private looked at me and asked, "First sergeant, what's a yardbird?" The question caught me off guard, because I hadn't intended to use the word. I didn't even know what it meant, but I had to come up with something fast so as not to look foolish.

I looked at him and said, "A yardbird is a bird that comes in and feeds out of your backyard. It depends on the owner of the yard to feed it. You're just like that yardbird because you have to depend on someone else just to eat." He gave me a strange look, and I told him to just take off.

After that, the word *yardbird* stuck in my mind. I couldn't forget it. I went home that night and got out Webster's dictionary and looked up *yard bird*.

The definition said it was, a "soldier assigned to a mental task or restricted to a limited area as a disciplinary measure; an untrained or inept enlisted man; one who is lacking in fitness or aptitude, unfit, not suitable to the time, place or occasion, inappropriate, often to absurd degree, lacking sense or reason, foolish, generally incompetent."

The various meanings in the definition amazed me. I had not known that this word had a military significance. I had never heard it before. I believed the word had been divinely put into my mouth to halt the swear words I had been using on the private, so I said, "Okay Lord, You help me with this. Instead of cussing at them, I'll call them yardbirds."

I had someone type the definition up for me. We had a bulletin board in the company and it was a mandatory rule in the army worldwide to read the company bulletin board three times a day, morning, noon and evening. I posted the definition of yardbird on the bulletin board. Instead of swearing at the soldiers, I started calling them yardbirds.

Somehow the men started coming up with marching cadence with the word *yardbird* in it. The word started to become popular in the company. I'd call all the privates yardbirds if they were messing up. Then one day I started having a private here and there come talk to me one on one. They would say, "First sergeant, cuss at me if you want, but please don't call me a yardbird." I chuckled to myself in private about that one. The men would suddenly rather be sworn at than to be called a yardbird.

The word yardbird started getting around in the unit. I noticed that other NCO's didn't cuss as much any more, even when we had meetings. I heard them calling their people yardbirds too, and they weren't swearing at them as much. The word began to replace swear words in the unit. To be called a yardbird was the lowest form of insult and a great dishonor. None of the soldiers wanted to be called a yardbird.

I knew this was a move of God. He had started out cleaning me up and turned it into a major clean up of the whole unit. Soon I no longer used the nasty, filthy, dirty words I once had and I thanked God for my deliverance.

Yardbird is the word I used then. As my walk with the Lord continued, that word yardbird left my vocabulary. I didn't cuss any more and I thanked God.

This was a season of direction and cleansing in my life. It was a time of plan and purpose that God initiated in me. I thank Him for that season because it was a time that I had much to be delivered from. One day at a time, He took this habit out of me, and another day He took that one out of me. I welcomed the work He was doing in me. I felt bad with all that garbage in me. I wanted to be delivered. I knew Jesus and who He was, and I knew that one of the reasons He came to earth was to provide deliverance.

The Spirit of the LORD *is upon Me, Because He*

has anointed Me To preach the gospel to the poor; He has sent Me to heal the brokenhearted, To proclaim liberty to the captives And recovery of sight to the blind, To set at liberty those who are oppressed; To proclaim the acceptable year of the LORD.   Luke 4:18, 19

Jesus came to set us free. He came to deliver all of mankind. He came to heal the brokenhearted. Thank God, He was willing to pay the supreme price to rescue us from all of our sins and bondages. All we have to do is call upon His name and He responds in power. People are healed and delivered. Their messed up lives are turned around. Jesus turned my messed up life around.

Back then I knew it didn't do any good to have the Word of God coming out of my mouth one minute and words of destruction coming out the next minute. I didn't want to look like a hypocrite. My life was changed. It was no longer all about me or my own wants and needs. It was about Jesus in me and people seeing Jesus in me.

Chapter Seven

BACK IN THE STATES

In 1985, my family and I were stationed back in the United States. Here the Lord would continue to teach me lessons on faith and trust. Some of those lessons were easier than other lessons, but they all produced fruit in my life and began to direct me down the path of my calling in God.

In November of that year, I had problems with the car. I was driving home from work when the engine started to lose power. I somehow managed to make it off the interstate when the car broke down completely. I pushed it off the road and popped the hood to check the engine, but I couldn't find anything wrong. It was about seven more miles to home and it was pouring down rain.

By this time I had seen the Lord answer so many of my prayers that I instinctively bowed my head and gave my predicament right over to him as I stood there alongside the road. I prayed and asked

Jesus to make the car start and run long enough to get me home. I got back in the car in faith and turned the key. The engine started up and ran like a champ all the way home with no more problems. I had prayed *believing* I already had my request fulfilled, and the Lord honored my faith.

Jesus tells us in His Word that this is how we are to pray. Too many believers don't understand the simple faith of a child that the Lord asks us to have. They complicate it with doubt and worry, but Jesus made it clear that faith was the key to unlocking the answers to our prayers.

> *Therefore I say to you, whatever things you ask when you pray, believe that you receive them, and you will have them.* Mark 11:24

On April 28, 1986, after our church's Good Friday service had ended, I felt led to talk to the pastor. I had felt led for months to talk to the pastor, but had not been able to get enough courage to talk with him.

The Lord was dealing with me on a remaining bondage I had. I wanted to quit smoking. After that service, I was drawn to the pastor like a magnetic force was pulling me. He walked out of the side door of the sanctuary. I walked out to the hallway and met up with him in one of the classrooms.

I told the pastor that I had been smoking for twenty-five years and I really felt led of the Lord to have him pray for deliverance for me. I told him I felt led of the Spirit that we should go to the altar, kneel down and pray. Bless the man, he didn't question or hesitate. We both went back inside to the altar, knelt down, and prayed.

As I walked out of the church that night, I felt something different. Each day I would cover myself with the blood of Jesus over my problem and claim the stripes of Jesus had healed me. At times I would get the urge to smoke, but I would fight it with the scriptures.

Whenever you're struggling to overcome some bondage in your life, you have to give the problem over to the Lord and He will help you. He knows the secret desires of your heart. If you're not sincere about wanting to be free, then you can't fool Him. He knows. But He also knows when you are serious. He'll help you, but you have to accept the deliverance you are praying for. Believe in it, and walk in great faith.

On June 11, 1986, I was running a two-mile course in the morning, which I had planned ahead of time in my mind. I came to the one-mile mark where I was supposed to turn around and start back, but I was led of the Lord to continue on ahead. I started praying, "Lord, tell me why should I continue running." The Lord simply urged me to go on.

Soon I passed the two-mile mark. I wanted to take the shortcut back to the gym, but I continued to run on. I prayed, "Lord, give me strength, motivation, determination and breath to make this run."

By the time I came to the four-mile mark, I was hot and my T-shirt was soaked with sweat. I wanted to stop. The Lord told me to continue on and follow this road. By now, I was pleading with Him to tell me why I was doing this. He said, "Put one foot in front of the other. Keep running. Keep going. Don't stop. The road will get hard, but keep pushing ahead. Don't go too close to the shoulder where you could stumble and fall, or you could hit the ruts and rocks. Stay on the road, but beware of detours — they are misleading. Ask for strength and you shall receive. I will guide you. Trust in Me. You will become tired, hot and sweaty, but trust in Me."

I kept running and I kept praying to Jesus for strength. To myself, I continued to ask, "Why should I run this far?" When I reached five miles, I heard the Lord say, "The babes in Christ are confused. There is strife, confusion, jealousy, bitterness, and worldly things going on in the Church. It's hard, but stay on the road. There will be times when you won't have a friend. People will not be there for you. You'll become discouraged. When that happens, start praying and believe that I will answer your prayers. Stand firm and look up. My Son Jesus is still the way, the truth and the life."

I got the message then, and I have never forgotten it. Perseverance is a necessary element of the Christian life. Those of us who live in the United States have adapted to a culture of easy living. We're used to fast food, instant this, and automatic that, but life in God's Kingdom doesn't work that way. Just like the military tests and tries men and women to prepare them for service, God tests and tries His people to prepare them for Kingdom living. No matter how hard it gets Jesus' followers need to keep putting one foot in front of the other, learning to persevere in spite of circumstances.

Unfortunately, too many Christians in the Church today are still babes in Christ. They don't know or understand the Word of God or how to live the Christian life. The Lord used the run I took that day to begin growing a burden in my heart for His babes. During this season in my life, the Lord began to prepare my heart for the call that our friend, Ellie, had prophesied over me back in Panama.

In August of 1986, I returned from a two-day road trip. I was in my PT uniform getting ready to go to the gym, but suddenly I didn't feel like going. Instead, I went to the motor pool to turn in the military vehicle I had been using.

I returned to the readiness group then where my sergeant major asked me if I could go on a particular mission. I agreed, and soon I was in route to Williamsport, Pennsylvania. The weather was bad. It was raining hard. I was watching the road and praying in my prayer language, when tears slowly started coming out of my eyes. I felt such sadness.

I said, "Lord, what is happening? Tell me, please, Lord." A rushing flow of chills moved through me mightily. The Lord said, "There are married people in the Church with problems and they are hurting. Husbands and wives are not listening to each other. They are playing a fifty-fifty game when they are supposed to be united as one together."

The Lord brought to my mind the scriptures in Genesis 2:18, 24.

> *It is not good for the man to live alone. I will make a helper suitable for him…. Man will leave his father and mother and be united to his wife, and they will become one flesh.* (NIV)

The Lord continued to speak to me. He said, "People have hurts, pains, bitterness, and confusion rooted deep in their hearts from striving with one another. Husbands and wives will not humble themselves towards each other. Tell the married couples to spend time together in the privacy of their homes, holding hands, looking at each other, and praying in one accord. Tell them that if they do not know what to pray about they should pray to Me and ask Me to flow through them. I will put the words into their mouths. Tell them to pray to loosen the spirit of pride out of each other, commanding it to go back to the powers of darkness. Tell them to pray for each other to be humble, listening to what one another has to say. Tell them to pray together as a family."

The Lord then laid the following scriptures on my heart,

The eyes of your understanding being enlightened; that you may know what is the hope of His calling, what are the riches of the glory of His inheritance in the saints, and what is the exceeding greatness of His power toward us who believe, according to the working of His mighty power which He worked in Christ when He raised Him from the dead and seated Him at His right hand in the heavenly places, far above all principality and power and might and dominion, and every name that is named, not only in this age but also in that which is to come. And He put all things under His feet, and gave Him to be head over all things to the church, which is His body, the fullness of Him who fills all in all.   Ephesians 1:18-23

Even when we were dead in trespasses, made us alive together with Christ (by grace you have been saved), and raised us up together, and made us sit together in the heavenly places in Christ Jesus, that in the ages to come He might show the exceeding riches of His grace in His kindness toward us in Christ Jesus. For by grace you have been saved through faith, and that not of yourselves; it is the gift of God, not of works, lest anyone should boast.   Ephesians 2:5-9

As the Lord gave me this message, I felt a hurt deep inside my heart. It was trying to root there and spread all through me. It was the kind of ache you feel on behalf of someone else who is messed up, lost, and hurting...a pain like the kind I felt when we lost our first son.

Rivers of tears ran down my face as I drove. I couldn't stop them. I prayed, "Thank You, Lord. Help me with this. I feel like I have to light the match to get the fire started. You know I don't want to get up and tell the church this, but for Your sake and because of what You went through to save me, I will do it."

One day not long after that happened, I was ushering at church. I was standing in the back as the praise and worship was going on when I heard the Lord tell me to go put my arm around an elderly gentleman who was there in the service. I asked the Lord to confirm this, because I wanted to be sure this was of Him and not something I thought of on my own. I prayed in the Spirit and after that a sister that I knew went up to another woman and put her arm around her. This was exactly what the Lord had asked me to do, and I took this as His confirmation.

I said, "Thank You, Lord," and moved toward the man. I put my arms around this brother, and I prayed in the Spirit as the congregation was singing. I could feel the hurt and the pain this man was feeling. The Lord put a word of comfort in my mouth for him, and I spoke on behalf of the Lord, saying, "I, the Lord, will take that root of pain from deep inside your heart. Just give it to Me."

The man simply said, "Oh, yes," and tears flowed

down his cheeks. I just gave him a big hug. I had been praying all morning for the Holy Spirit to move in the church service, not knowing that the Spirit would choose to move in me to touch someone.

I had learned to feel the hurts of others the same way God felt them. The burden that He had put into my heart was now leading me into ministering to others as the Spirit led. There was so much the Lord was saying to me, and I knew I couldn't keep these things to myself for long. Soon He would ask me to begin to step out into the call He had placed on my life. He had worked to clean me up on the inside, and soon He would work to clean up some others in my house, in order to prepare me for a life of full-time ministry.

Chapter Eight

THE PRODIGAL

On December 19, 1987, my wife hurt her legs in an accident that was directly caused by our son Joe. Our son took off in his car, and I took my wife to the hospital. A few days later while I was visiting her in the hospital, she asked me to find Joe. I promised her I would find him.

At home, I decided to write a letter to the members of my family. I sent a copy of the following letter to each one of them.

To my family,

I love every one of you. Writing this letter is something I feel I have to do. I hope you will keep this letter private within our family.

Mom and Dad, you live five miles from my home. Sister and husband, you live ten miles from my home. Brother and wife, you live seven miles from my home. The entire length of my Army career, I have never lived this close to home.

I love Edna dearly. We are committed to each other through sickness and health, till death do us part. She is a good wife and mother to put up with me all these years, and even more so because I am in the military. I want to leave this state so bad I can taste it, but not yet.

When I accepted Jesus Christ as my Lord and Savior, He already had missions for my family and me. Accept Christ Jesus as your Lord and Savior. Don't worry about anything, but in all your prayers ask God for what you need. Always ask Him with a thankful heart and God's peace, which is far beyond human understanding, will keep your hearts and minds safe in union with Christ Jesus.

We all have faults, but when you have Jesus, He will help clean you up. He is still working on me.

Brother-in-law, I know how you feel, and I pray for you daily. About your mom and dad, ask God to help you — you can't do it alone. Give up the alcohol and visit your mom and dad. We only live a short life on this earth.

On December 19, 1987 at 8:30 PM, my son who knows Jesus Christ as Savior walked away from Him, although I believe it will only be for a short season. When he ran out of the house, we tried to stop him, and he caused the accident that injured my wife. Edna is in the hospital. She will be operated on Monday. In spite of all the pain that Edna is in, she still loves him. It's hard, but I love him, too. I still have the peace and understanding that God through His Son, Jesus Christ, sends to us through prayer and the Holy Spirit.

I pray for you all that you come out of the world, read the Bible, believe every word and accept Jesus Christ as your Lord and Savior. I know He is coming shortly. I want to see all of you in Heaven with our Lord Jesus and His Father.

Please pray for my family and me.

Love,
Dereick

After I sent the letter, I got into my car with the intention of looking for Joe. I rode around aimlessly for a short time, then I prayed to Jesus, "Lord, send me in the right direction." I headed over to his girlfriend's house. I prayed, "Lord, help me find our son." I knew I was facing a spiritual battle ahead of me to get my son back from the enemy, and I used God's Word as my weapon. I prayed Isaiah 54:17 over both Joe and myself.

No weapon formed against you shall prosper, And every tongue which rises against you in judgment You shall condemn. This is the heritage of the

> *servants of the* LORD, *And their righteousness is*
> *from Me," Says the* LORD. Isaiah 54:17

As I pulled up in front of his girlfriend's house, God only knows that I didn't want to go knock on the door. I just couldn't think of the right words to say. In my helplessness, I asked the Lord for the words, and in faith, I got out of the car and went to the door. I thought that her mother would answer the door. No one came when I knocked, so I rang the doorbell, thinking that maybe no one could hear my knock.

To my surprise, my son's girlfriend answered the door herself. I hadn't expected to face her. I knew this could only be God's hand working things His way. I was short for words at first and prayed silently that the Lord would tell me what to say.

I asked her, "Have you seen my son?"

She said, "Yes, he's okay". Moving to one side, she opened the door and gestured for me to enter. "It's cold out. Come on in. My mom and I have been talking to him and telling him to go home."

Inside, I told her that I had done a lot of praying since the night of the incident. My flesh had wanted to call the police and press charges. But I knew he would be picked up for hit-and-run and have a record, maybe even sent to a juvenile home. I told her how I had prayed, "Lord, help me. Give me peace," and the Lord had done just that, so I had not called the police. That would have only made matters worse.

"I love my son," I finally said to her. "We all make mistakes. We're human beings. I just hope it's not a costly mistake. When you know Jesus Christ as Lord and Savior, you can give all your problems to Him and He will see you through. We have to believe and walk in faith."

Like with most teenagers, I was having a hard time really communicating with her. I wanted to understand her, to listen to what she was going through, just like I wanted to understand Joe.

I asked her then, "Do you love my son?"

She shrugged her shoulders. "I don't know. I get mixed up."

"Does Joe love you?"

She said, "Yes, he tells me all the time."

"Anybody can say they love you," I told her, "but real love is what someone does for you. It means more than just words."

She was silent, thinking about what I had said.

"I love my son. Please tell Joe that I won't discipline him. I don't understand what's going on with him. I want to try to understand him, love him and help him. Tell him that my doors are open for him." I added, "They're open for you, too. I know you're afraid to come over to our home, but my doors are open. Don't be scared. I want to understand."

I left the girlfriend's home. I still hadn't found Joe, but the visit had not been wasted. I believed things would soon be different between the girl and Edna and me.

I started to go in the direction of my son's school. Sitting at the red light waiting to turn left toward the school, I asked the Lord, "Which way should I go?" I was headed to where logic said would be the right way. But when the light turned green, I automatically turned right and went up the road toward Enola. I thought, *Lord, this is You.* As I was going up the hill, to my surprise I saw what looked like Joe's yellow Volkswagen. I thought, *This can't be.*

We went right by each other — there he was. He even waved at me. I was in shock. I checked my mirrors quickly. No cars were coming either way, so I made a U-turn right there in the road. I went down the road a little further, but when I couldn't see him I started thinking he had turned off somewhere. Then, all at once, I saw the yellow Volkswagen waiting at the red light where I had been sitting earlier.

I followed him, thinking that he wasn't going to stop anywhere that I could catch up. But Joe fooled me. He went directly to his girlfriend's house, pulled over and stopped the car. I pulled in right behind him. He got out of the Volkswagen and looked at me, not moving.

I got out of the car and walked toward him. He just stood there, waiting. As I came near him, I reached out my hand, hoping desperately that he would do the same. He did. We shook hands. The moment was filled with a feeling so great that only our Lord Jesus could understand it. We stood there in the road just looking at each other. I was lost for words.

A man pulled his car up somewhere near by and his two dogs jumped out and ran over to us. I reached down to pet them. Looking at my son, I said to the dogs, "Go to your master." The double meaning of my words rippled between us. The dogs ran back to their owner.

Joe looked at me and I looked at him. We both knew what my words had really meant: "Go to your Master." We had both committed our lives to serving our Master, our Lord Jesus. No matter what lay ahead for us as a family, we would have only peace and joy if we entrusted our situation over to Him. In Jesus, we would have a great victory.

For twenty long years, I had prepared for war—war the way that men fought it. But this day, I had prepared for a different kind of war—a spiritual war—and I had won. I had gone to battle with the most powerful weapons man has ever seen or known: the Word of God and the blood of the Lamb who was slain at Calvary.

Chapter Nine

HOLDING ONTO THE PROMISE

One day in 2001, we received a phone call from our daughter-in-law, Dereick's wife, stating that she was taking him to Holy Spirit hospital in Camp Hill, Pennsylvania. He was ill with a severe migraine headache. She told us that Dereick was saying he thought he was going to die.

The enemy has tried to take out our son, Dereick, many times, but God gave us a promise many years ago that we have believed in and stood firmly upon throughout our days as parents. When we lost our one son at the age of three many years ago, God promised us He would not let the enemy take another one of our children. Therefore, we were able to bring that promise before Him any time something happened to any of our children.

On the way to the hospital, we remembered the promise that God has given us. We joined hands as we were driving and went before the Lord with the promise He had given us. Any time anything was wrong where our children were concerned, we would remind God of His promise to us—the enemy would never be allowed to take another one of our children.

As we finished our prayer, we were getting onto the expressway. Suddenly the car began to shake and rock back and forth from right to left and left to right. It felt just like a jet was flying very low and sounded like a gust of loud wind flying right over us. In fact, we both started looking around for this jet, but there wasn't any to be seen anywhere. Suddenly, we both thought of the same explanation at once. We looked at one another and said "Oh my God" at the same time. We realized that it could only have been an angel flying by us.

When we got to the hospital and went to be with Dereick and his wife, we realized that the angel was already there. We believed it because of what had happened in the car and because of the promise God had given us. The doctors already had hooked our son up to an IV, and they were beginning to deal with his illness.

Later, one day we were watching a tape by Jesse Duplantis. We sat up in surprise when Jesse described the very same sound we had heard that day on the way to the hospital. He'd had a very similar experience and also attributed it to an angel flying by. We took that as confirmation. We knew an angel had flown by our car to go rescue our son. We give God glory for that because He is a faithful God who always keeps His promises.

Chapter Ten

A VISION OF ANGELS

In 1990, I was driving a truck across the South Street Bridge on Interstate 83 in Harrisburg, Pennsylvania. It was about 2:45 AM. As I crossed, I looked out the right side of the vehicle and saw a vision. As far as my eyes could see, there stood a multitude of angels all lined up shoulder to shoulder. They were so bright. They glowed radiantly. It was so awesome.

Suddenly a multitude of horses marched up, their hoofs clicking smartly all in unison. The horses, all together, moved right beside the angels and stopped in unison. Then the angels all simultaneously mounted the horses. At once, the horses began to advance and soon were moving at a gallop. Again, all movement was done in unison.

I saw the angels' right arms cross over in front of them and each one reached down to pull a saber out of the scabbard. Their scabbards were on their left and as they pulled the sabers free they moved simultaneously to lift the sabers high in their right hands.

As they lifted the sabers high, I could see on the first saber brilliant gold letters that read "Glory to God in the Highest." And the Lord let me see that there were swords as far as my eyes could see. All of the sabers had written right down the middle between the two sharp edges "Glory to God in the Highest."

The horses started to move quickly forward in a charging position. And the angels' right arms with sabers in hand swung high behind their heads and they all shouted in one accord, "Glory to God in the highest." As they shouted this, something sounding like a roaring thunder came my way. It was so loud and such a thundering voice that it shook the truck I was driving. I could even feel the vibration ripple through my body.

The angels rode the horses at full gallop, and as they swung their swords forward, lightning burst forth out of the tip of every sword. They pulled the swords back in behind them again to swing them forward again, and on like this they continued, swinging those sabers back and forward. Every time they slashed down with the swords they shouted, "Glory to God in the highest!"

I had no idea what they were battling in front of them, but I knew they were fighting something, and it was a furious battle because they kept charging and moving forward, slashing whatever was in front of them. All of a sudden, the vision stopped and I said, "Lord what are the angels fighting in front of them?"

Suddenly, the vision came back, and the Lord showed me that to the front of the angels was nothing but darkness. I mean it was a black darkness, and every time the angels slashed forward, shouting, lightning bolts shot out of the sword tips tearing into that darkness. The scene was so awesome. The lightning bolts cut into that darkness, and every time they made a cut they made light, and every time they made light there was less darkness.

Because of the vastness of the darkness, the angels kept fighting and slicing into it, charging forward and roaring with every slash of their swords "Glory to God in the highest." And they continued fighting it endlessly and with no interruption and no wavering. Together they moved continuously in unison.

I asked the Lord, "What is this darkness?"

He said to me, "Son, that is the darkness in the area where you are right now. That is how dark it is, filled with all kinds of evil and ungodliness. Even in the churches, in the pastors, and in the ones who say they are My saints. Darkness is in a lot of them, and they all need to repent and seek deliverance." Then the Lord brought this scripture to my mind,

"Get up, sanctify the people, and say, 'Sanctify yourselves for tomorrow, because thus says the

> Lᴏʀᴅ God of Israel: *"There is an accursed thing*
> *in your midst, O Israel; you cannot stand before*
> *your enemies until you take away the accursed*
> *thing from among you." ' "*
>
> Joshua 7:13

He said, "Most of the area you are in is in this darkness. A principality has come into the area. The people are so desensitized to it that they don't even realize they are desensitized."

Then the Lord said, "My angels are fighting that principality. While I have sent men to subdue the earth, My angels have been sent to fight principalities. You are to subdue the earth and do what I tell you to do." Then I recalled these scriptures,

> *Then God blessed them, and God said to them,*
> *"Be fruitful and multiply; fill the earth and subdue*
> *it; have dominion over the fish of the sea, over the*
> *birds of the air, and over every living thing that*
> *moves on the earth."*
>
> Genesis 1:28

> *You will not need to fight in this battle. Position*
> *yourselves, stand still and see the salvation of the*
> Lᴏʀᴅ, *who is with you, O Judah and Jerusalem!'*
> *Do not fear or be dismayed; tomorrow go out*
> *against them, for the* Lᴏʀᴅ *is with you.*
>
> 2 Chronicles 20:17

Then the vision stopped, and I woke up at the exit. The exit sign directed drivers to Camp Hill to go straight and those going to York to take the Interstate 83 South ramp. I was to get off at this ramp. But I didn't remember getting off. I didn't even remember driving the truck, yet somehow my truck got off at that exit!

I sat in awe behind the steering wheel at the exit sign. It seemed like someone else had driven the truck here. It didn't seem possible that I could have done it. The Lord had to have placed an angel into the truck to drive. I knew the vision was right from the Lord. It was an awesome vision, one that I never forgot.

We are going to fight this battle here on earth and win it through worship and prayer. God is helping us win the battle in the Harrisburg area where I live. He has allowed the darkness and the desolate area I saw to exist so that we can see His glory.

Everything we go through is to glorify the Lord. The people of Bethany in the New Testament stood around and wondered why Jesus didn't heal Lazarus before he died. Jesus explained to them that God had allowed Lazarus' death because He wanted the people to see His Glory. God works the same way today.

Just imagine a train at the end of town and the engine is humming. It's getting ready to come down the track. It is coming with all the glory of God, and Jesus is the conductor. The price of tickets was paid for by the blood of Jesus for all men to get on the glory train to eternal life. God is at the end of town waiting with engines humming to come with all His glory, so we might know that He is the God of the area where we live.

He is the God who is going to subdue the darkness. When we send up our worship through radical praise, radical fasting and radical standing on the promises of God, He will display His glory. When the enemy comes, it's always in an effort to deceive us. But the Spirit of truth is raising up a standard so that we might win this battle in this area for the glory of God. We must stand and go forth in the name of the Lord because He is the Lord of hosts.

Jesus leads all of God's armies and is fighting this battle on our behalf. We only need to subdue the earth where we live and stand strong, holding ground until the Lord brings His mighty heavenly armies. They will come, displaying all of God's might and glory.

My wife and I are now pastoring a church in the Harrisburg area. We started this church on July 28 2001. God spoke to us several years ago to start a church. When we started the church, my wife looked at me and said, "What are we going to name this church?"

When I prayed about it, God took me back to the vision and He showed the name to me as clear and as plain as He had in 1990. God showed me the angels' swords and words written on them. Those words were, "Glory to God in the Highest." And the Lord said to me, "This is what you are to name the church — Glory to God in the Highest Ministries Church."

And so, in obedience to God, we now pastor a church called Glory to God in the Highest. Hallelujah! Hallelujah! We began meeting in a motel, and six months later God had blessed us so much that we were able to move into a building.

Chapter Eleven

ANOTHER VISION

In June 2002, my father went home to be with the Lord. My father was a believer in the Lord Jesus and we were confident that he had gone to be in a much better place.[1]

About six months after that, my wife and I were driving to church on a Sunday morning. As we went, I suddenly had a vision as I was driving. I saw my dad walking along holding someone else's hand. The other person looked to be a small child. The Lord then revealed to me that this child I was seeing was our three-year-old son, whom we had lost many years before. He had drowned not long after I had joined the military.

My father and our small son were walking together in what looked to be a very beautiful place. Then suddenly I saw a dog running around them in circles, playing. I recognized the dog. It was Duster, the dog we had for years before we received orders to go overseas. My parents had kept that dog for us after we left and he had passed away while we were overseas.

Then I saw another dog come into the vision, chasing Duster, and this was a dog we owned after we came back to the United States. It was a little poodle named Shadow. The two animals were playing together like dogs do, and they were running circles around my dad and our son.

As I saw all of these things taking place in my vision—the dogs playing, my father and son walking together hand-in-hand—I began to weep. I wept uncontrollably, thanking God for allowing me to see that my loved ones were together and happy. The vision gave me tremendous peace and comfort. I thank God for that and I thank God for caring for me so much that He would reach down to comfort me in my grief at losing my father. It was a very real reminder of how much God loves all of us. Glory to God in the highest.

[1]*We are confident, yes, well pleased rather to be absent from the body and to be present with the Lord* (2 Corinthians 5:8)

Chapter Twelve

THE SHOFAR

Several years ago, the Lord gave my wife a teaching for our congregation about the shofar. The blowing of the shofar has great significance in spiritual warfare. Each time that a "trumpet" is mentioned in the Old Testament, that word is really referring to a shofar, or a ram's horn.

Joshua and the Israelites used shofars at Jericho on the last day of their march around that city. In the book of Judges, Gideon used shofars to scatter and overcome the enemies of God, who outnumbered them greatly. In both of these examples, God instructed these men to use shofars and when to blow them. (See Joshua 6 and Judges 7.)

After word of my wife's teaching got around, several ministers in the area approached us about blowing the shofar over the city. We decided to do it, so we planned a trip to the highest area in Harrisburg's Reservoir Park. At the highest peak of the park, you can see miles out from the north, south, east and west of the city. We went there and blew the shofar, and we interceded for the state of Pennsylvania for twenty-one days.

This time was not our first knowledge of the shofar. The Lord gave me a longing to blow the shofar many years earlier while I was still in the military. The first time I heard the sound of the shofar was 1969. Our unit deployed overseas to the country of Turkey. Then we were linking up with the Turkish paratroopers, and we were scheduled to jump on a drop zone one mile wide and two miles long. It was the largest mass jump of troopers and equipment since WWII. In nearly every town and village that we passed on the way to our objective, someone was blowing a shofar at certain times of the day. At that time, I had no idea what that was all about, and little did I know that I was predestined to blow the shofar myself one day as pastor of a church.

After the Lord introduced me to the shofar, another pastor, along with five other gentlemen, my wife and myself went to the State Capitol building in Harrisburg. There were two of us who had shofars. One had a small ram's horn and another gentlemen had a regular trumpet. We had been invited by one of the state senators, who was a friend of the pastor we were with, to blow the shofar at the Capitol building.

As we were walking past the senate floor, Catherine Baker-Knoll, the lieutenant governor of the Commonwealth of Pennsylvania, came out and saw us. She invited us to go onto the Senate floor. We went inside the Senate talking with her casually, and she asked that we blow the shofar on the Senate floor. We blew our shofars on the Senate floor and she was astonished at how loud and strong the sound rang through the room.

Afterwards we fellowshipped with the senator who had invited us there. He guided eight of us to the top of the Capitol dome. Outside the dome, we prayed and blew the shofar toward the north, south, east and west over Harrisburg while my wife interceded in prayer on the landing below us. After blowing the shofar, the Holy Spirit gave one of the gentlemen a scripture, which he read aloud.

Blow the trumpet in Zion, Consecrate a fast, Call a sacred assembly; Gather the people, Sanctify the congregation, Assemble the elders, Gather the children and nursing babes; Let the bridegroom go out from his chamber, And the bride from her dressing room. Let the priests, who minister to the LORD, Weep between the porch and the altar; Let them say, "Spare Your people, O LORD, And do not give Your heritage to reproach, That the nations should rule over them. Why should they say among the peoples, 'Where is their God?'" Then the Lord will be zealous for His land, And pity His people. The LORD will answer and say to His people, "Behold, I will send you grain and new wine and oil, and you will be satisfied by them; I will no longer make you a reproach among the nations. But I will remove far from you the northern army, And will drive him away into a barren and desolate land, With his face toward the eastern sea And his back toward the western sea; His stench will come up, And his foul odor will rise, Because he has done monstrous things." Fear not, O land; Be glad and rejoice, for the LORD has done marvelous things! Do not be afraid, you beasts of the field; For the open pastures are springing up, And the tree bears its fruit; The fig tree and the vine yield their strength. Be glad then, you children of Zion, And rejoice in the LORD your God; For He has given you the former rain faithfully, And He will cause the rain to come down for you; The former rain, And the latter rain in the first month. The threshing floors shall be full of wheat, And the vats shall overflow with new wine and oil. "So I will restore to you the years that the swarming locust has eaten, The crawling locust, The consuming locust, And the chewing locust, My great army which I sent among you. You shall eat in plenty and be satisfied, And praise the name of the LORD your God, Who has dealt wondrously with you; And My people shall never be put to shame. Then you shall know that I am in the midst of Israel: I am the LORD your God And there is no other. My people shall never be put to shame. And it shall come to pass afterward That I will pour out My Spirit on all flesh; Your sons and your daughters shall prophesy, Your old men shall dream dreams, Your young men shall see visions. And also on My menservants and on My maidservants I will pour out My Spirit in those days. Joel 2:15-29

After the blowing of the shofar, we went to the senator's office to pray.

The following month, our pastor friend invited my wife and me to come alongside him as armor bearers while he served as the Senate chaplain at the state capitol meeting. My wife and I accompanied him and on the Senate floor, and we were asked by Lieutenant Governor Catherine Baker-Knoll to sit beside her on the Senate floor, instead of in the gallows where guests would normally sit.

After the Senate meeting was over, the lieutenant governor escorted our friend, my wife and me to her office and we had prayer together. The lieutenant governor received a word from the Lord. Her assistant also received prayer and unknowingly felt the anointing of the Holy Spirit.

In our church services, we use the shofar intently during the service. It's certainly scriptural to do so.[1] I blow it before the service and during the service. If I feel led, I just blow the shofar. I believe what the Bible says about the shofar, and I believe it is a symbol of power, strength and defense. Traditionally, it's one of the most powerful weapons the Lord uses. The shofar breaks down spiritual walls and snaps the chains of bondage.[2]

A shofar is made from the horn of a goat, a ram, or an antelope. The shofar I have used is made from an African antelope horn, and it was made in Israel.

Every time you see the word *horn* in the Bible it represents power and when it's used in reference to the Lord, it refers to the shofar. When you blow the shofar, you are penetrating the air, the realm from which Satan rules. Satan hates the sound of the shofar because it penetrates the darkness with the power and light of God. It confuses and scatters the enemies of God.

The Hebrew word *shofar* comes from the word, which means, "hollowness, breathe into it, you have life." In ancient Jewish tradition, if the shofar is not sounded at the beginning of the New Year, evil will occur at the end of it, because the accuser, Satan, has not been confused.

The sword of the Lord is the shofar—God sets ambushes with the shofar. Glory hallelujah!

[1]*With trumpets and the sound of a horn; Shout joyfully before the LORD, the King* (Psalm 98:6).

[2]*The adversaries of the LORD shall be broken in pieces; From heaven He will thunder against them. The LORD will judge the ends of the earth. "He will give strength to His king, And exalt the horn of His anointed"* (1 Samuel 2:10).

Chapter Thirteen

DREAMS FROM THE LORD

In the past year or more, I have been having some dreams from the Lord. While I've had them throughout my Christian life, in this particular season I've had more than I normally have. The Lord has been showing me various people in these dreams, and when I have them it's as though I am being translated in the Spirit to where they are, hearing their conversations and what's going on around them. Several weeks after the dreams have passed, my wife and I will be ministering to different people in church service when the dreams come back to me and I'm able to minister to these people based on what took place in the dreams.

I've also had some dreams that speak a particular message about what's on God's heart, especially about the moves of the Spirit to come.

In March of 2001, I had a dream. I saw a group of children between the ages of six and twelve going into their homes. As they went into their homes, some got into the cupboards in the kitchen and took out a bottle of cooking oil. Some went into their parents' room and came out with bottles of oil.

These children took the oil into their schools and anointed the desks and doors. I saw one child go into the rest room and anoint the sinks and the doorway. Another child went into the library and walked up and down the aisles anointing the books on the shelves. Another child walked around the principal's and administrative offices, anointing the doorways and counters.

This went on for hours until later at lunch all these children sat down together in the cafeteria. I heard them talking about the areas in the school that each had anointed. One of them had even anointed the flagpole in the parking lot. I was in awe upon hearing about everything they had anointed. As the children talked, I realized that they had anointed the whole school. No one child had known what the others were doing until they began talking about it.

I asked the Lord, "What's this all about? What is going to take place? Are You going to speak to this generation to have them anoint that school because something was going to happen and You are going to prevent it?" I had no idea, so I set it aside in my mind and my heart, although I did talk to my wife about it.

In March 2004, I had another dream and in it I saw a girl who looked familiar. She looked just like a girl in our church whose mother is one of our elders. The girl from our church is named Ashley, and the girl who was in my dream looked like her. I saw this girl standing there and a couple of other girls came over to join her.

The girl who looked like Ashley said, "I have a secret." One of the other girls asked her what her secret was. "Ashley" told her that she would have to be born again before she could tell her the secret. The second girl responded that she was born again. "Ashley" then asked her, in order to test if what she was saying was true, "What makes you born again?" The girl told her what she believed being born again meant, and "Ashley" said that she was correct. So "Ashley" told her the secret.

Before they knew it, other girls came over and they shared with them that they had a secret. The other girls wanted to know the secret also, and they were also asked if they knew what it meant to be born again. But these girls were not born again and did not know what it meant. "Ashley" and her friend who already knew the secret then led these new girls through a prayer of salvation.

Afterward, "Ashley" realized that all the girls around them wanted to know the secret, so she told them all. "The Lord told me to anoint the school. If you want to help, what you need to do is go home and get some oil. Then bring it to school tomorrow, and we will anoint this school."

The next day the children came with different

sizes and bottles of oil with them to school. "Ashley" had them gather around with their oil and she prayed over the oil.

She prayed, "In the name of the Father, Son and Holy Ghost and by the authority of Jesus, we are anointing this school that no weapon formed against us shall prosper."

She told them no harm would come to them and nothing would happen to any of the children or the teachers. The Lord would send angels to guard and protect the school. She told them to go to their classrooms and anoint everything. They should anoint wherever they went inside the school. So the children went to their classes, and they anointed the desks, chalkboards, teachers' desks, principal's office, doorways, and rest rooms…whatever they could.

After school ended they came together and held hands and prayed. "Ashley," who was the leader of this anointing, gave them more instructions. She told them they needed to talk about Jesus with friends, relatives, parents or anyone they played with. She told them that whoever calls on the name of Jesus would be saved and if they had never asked Jesus Christ to be their Savior they needed to ask Him right then and now.

She said, "We have to tell the children. We have to start someplace. If we don't tell them and they don't get saved, then they will go to hell. We have to tell them because they are our friends. We can pray a prayer like this: 'Dear God, I thank you for loving me so much that you sent your Son to die for my sins. I admit that I need Your love and forgiveness. I believe that Jesus paid for my sins and died on the cross, and I receive Him by faith as my personal Savior. I accept the gift of salvation as my own.'"

She told them that when they pray for other children that it had to be from their heart. She encouraged them to ask the Lord to touch them and give them the right words to say. God would hear their prayers, she assured them, and He would forgive their sins and give them the gift of salvation. She also told them they needed to find a Bible at home and begin to learn to read it. She told them if they were already going to church that they could come to her church or they should find a good Bible-believing church.

My dream ended there, and I woke up in awe again. I started thinking about how God could have such a move of the Spirit through this young generation. I began talking to the Lord and asking Him the reason for the dream. Was it because the older generation was not being obedient or doing His will? Was this young generation coming up going to be like a Joshua generation? Would He have them "cross the Jordan" and go into a new land? Was there going to be a Promised Land full of milk and honey for this younger generation?

I believe the Lord is going to do this. I believe the

Lord is doing something so great and so mighty that it will blow the older generation away. Even the Bible scholars, preachers, teachers, evangelists and apostles are going to be blown away by God's awesome move on the younger generation.

I prayed to the Lord that I would do right and be a part of the move in the younger generation. I promised that my wife and I would do whatever He asked us to help in this vision so that He would touch our hearts also. I asked the Lord to give us the sermons, knowledge, insight, understanding and most of all wisdom that we would need to be obedient to Him in fulfilling our part of His plan.

The Lord said to me that His people were "strange" and "peculiar." Some of them would seemingly do things that were out of the ordinary, but when they were doing "a God thing" the Body of Christ would know it.

To understand all of this, I remembered a time in my own life when I was younger. I didn't have a full understanding of the Lord's ways then, and the Lord used a pastor to anoint me with oil for a healing. I realized then there was something about the anointing oil. I knew that you had to have faith to believe in order for healing to occur. My healing came because of my faith.

I started reading the Old Testament to find out where the use of oil started. As I read in the Word about all of the times anointing oil was used, I asked the Lord how strong that oil was and how powerful was it. I never forgot what the Lord told me about the anointing oil.

The Lord told me that this anointing oil was so great and so powerful that if the anointing left this earth and went into the clouds it would have a tremendous force of power and energy. If the anointing continued upward, leaving the earth's atmosphere and going off into space, it would still have enough energy and power to go into the next closest galaxy. It would travel faster than we could ever imagine, and it would leave that galaxy and go out into space where it would hit all the galaxies. Eventually, it could go all the way through space with force and energy to spare, and it would continue to go on for eons and eons, forever and ever, clear into infinity.

I stood there stunned unable to move. I thought about all the Lord had said about the oil. The human mind simply can't comprehend how great and powerful it was and still is. Oil that is set aside for God's purposes to anoint in power has enough energy to do anything He wants it to.

I said to Him then, "Lord, you can anoint me. Anoint me with that oil, and I'll receive whatever you want to give me." I told the Lord that I had faith enough for this and no one can take away what He told me. You see, man can say you're an idiot, a fool, that you talk like a child or that you're living in a storybook fantasy, but man's opinions are meaningless. Only what God says has any significance or power, because only what God says is truth.

God can speak only truth. That's why, when God says you are born again, you really do have a new life. If you've never experienced the new birth, you can turn to His Word to read about it. Jesus first taught about being born again in the book of John, chapter 3. Let's look at it here.

There was a man of the Pharisees named Nicodemus, a ruler of the Jews. This man came to Jesus by night and said to Him, "Rabbi, we know that You are a teacher come from God; for no one can do these signs that You do unless God is with him." Jesus answered and said to him, "Most assuredly, I say to you, unless one is born again, he cannot see the kingdom of God." Nicodemus said to Him, "How can a man be born when he is old? Can he enter a second time into his mother's womb and be born?" Jesus answered, "Most assuredly, I say to you, unless one is born of water and the Spirit, he cannot enter the kingdom of God. "That which is born of the flesh is flesh, and that which is born of the Spirit is spirit. "Do not marvel that I said to you, 'You must be born again.' The wind blows where it wishes, and you hear the sound of it, but cannot tell where it comes from and where it goes. So is everyone who is born of the Spirit. Nicodemus answered and said to Him, "How can these things be?" Jesus answered and said to him, "Are you the teacher of Israel, and do not know these things? "Most assuredly,

I say to you, We speak what We know and testify what We have seen, and you do not receive Our witness. "If I have told you earthly things and you do not believe, how will you believe if I tell you heavenly things? No one has ascended to heaven but He who came down from heaven, that is, the Son of Man who is in heaven. And as Moses lifted up the serpent in the wilderness, even so must the Son of Man be lifted up, that whoever believes in Him should not perish but have eternal life. For God so loved the world that He gave His only begotten Son, that whoever believes in Him should not perish but have everlasting life. For God did not send His Son into the world to condemn the world, but that the world through Him might be saved. He who believes in Him is not condemned; but he who does not believe is condemned already, because he has not believed in the name of the only begotten Son of God. And this is the condemnation, that the light has come into the world, and men loved darkness rather than light, because their deeds were evil. For everyone practicing evil hates the light and does not come to the light, lest his deeds should be exposed. But he who does the truth comes to the light, that his deeds may be clearly seen, that they have been done in God." John 3:1-21

You can also read about being born again in the book of First Peter.

Being born again, not of corruptible seed, but of incorruptible, by the word of God, which liveth and abideth for ever. For all flesh is as grass, and all the glory of man as the flower of grass. The grass withereth, and the flower thereof falleth away: But the word of the Lord endureth for ever. And this is the word which by the gospel is preached unto you.　　　1 Peter 1:23-25, KJV

Chapter Fourteen

Testimonies

The following stories are true-life testimonies of some of the members of Glory to God in the Highest Church. I hope that these testimonies will encourage and uplift you as you get to know each of these special people.

Testimonies to encourage others because of the vision that God has given to start the church, these are some of the testimonies of the work that God has done in the members lives.

Jose Aponte

Where can I even begin to tell my story when God has done so much in my life? I didn't even know God or that He was a protector until I came to know Pastors Dereick and Edna Smith.

I guess the best thing for me to do is start from the beginning. As I was a young boy, my mother took us kids to the church she had grown up in. I used to teach a Sunday school class at that church as a little boy, not knowing that God was preparing me even back then.

Life was good until my father left my mother. That's when life as I knew it took an entirely different turn. I was about twelve years old when this happened. When my dad left, it was like all the members of our family went their separate ways. My mom lost all control of us. She did her best, but in the end, it wasn't good enough. I found myself on the streets at that age doing what I had to do to get by. I stole from cars, sold drugs, and started hanging around with a gang, one of the worst gangs in Lancaster at that time.

At the age of thirteen, I was in a drug deal that went sour, and ended up getting shot. God's grace was on me then, and I didn't even realize it. Many things happened to me while I was running the streets. I was stabbed and even hit by a car. Needless to say, I did a lot of time in juvenile detention centers.

When I turned eighteen, I went to jail. I didn't know what real life was. I tried to commit suicide twice and found myself in a mental institution at one point of my life. To hear all of that now, a lot of people would think "Wow," but now that I know Jesus as my Savior, I look at those years as preparation for the work that God wants me to do for Him.

I've known Pastors Dereick and Edna Smith for

four years now. I remember the first day I walked into the Howard Johnson hotel for my first church service. I sat with my girlfriend in the back by the door because I wanted to be able to get out of there quick, but God had other plans. I had been to churches before, but I had never seen the Spirit of God move like I did that day. For the very first time in my life, I saw the power of God.

I sat there listening to the praise and worship music, but right before the preaching was to start, I got up to sneak out the back. From the front, Pastor Edna called out and stopped me, asking if I had a minute. Until this day, I praise God for humbling me, and I turned around and walked to the front. I could have never been prepared for what happened next. The Lord spoke through the pastors and laid out my whole life in front of the congregation. I stood there in tears. I knew then who God was for the first time in my life. For the pastors to know all that they did, it could only have been God.

Now, I'm living a Christ-filled life, but it hasn't been easy. There have been many times that I came very close to quitting. Every time I get to that point, God moves. I have to rely on God to see me through. Even as I write this, I'm facing difficulties that are trying to take me down. Just recently my boss fired me over an assumption. Now, I could have chosen to turn my back on God, but what good will that do? It's in difficult times that I must hold onto Him even more.

The enemy will keep on throwing things at you to see where your faith lies, just like the story of Job. He lost everything, but didn't lose his faith. God blessed him with even more than he had before.

I've learned through the teaching of this ministry how to keep my faith strong. God has made Himself known to me in many ways. One Saturday at a men's fellowship meeting, I was fed up with my life and all the pain I've experienced. I walked into the church and up to Pastor Dereick and asked for prayer. As he prayed for me, I could feel the hands of God surrounding me and holding me in comfort.

There was also a time at a Thursday night prayer meeting that I finally died to my flesh so that my spirit could grow stronger. As this happened, I could literally feel lashes on my back. It felt like open gashes were burning in my flesh like freshly opened cuts. Pastor Dereick explained to me that as I died to flesh, because of the desire of my heart and the love I have for Jesus, I was able to experience some of what Jesus felt. That was so awesome and profound to me. God is so good. He's heard all of my prayers and has caught many of my tears. He's answered many of my prayers already in the short time I've been coming to this ministry. For instance, I've prayed for my wife to be become an awesome woman of God and after much prayer and fasting, my wife is becoming a new person and our marriage is better than I could have ever imagined.

God has done so much more in my life than these

things that I couldn't possibly explain it all. To go into more detail would be for me to write my own book. I consider it an honor and a privilege to have shepherds like Pastors Dereick and Edna Smith. To me, they are like the mother and father that I never had. I can't wait to see what else God has in store for the ministry, for my marriage and for my life.

In being patient to wait on God and submissive to those in authority, God has been able to open my eyes to many things. I was bound to the court systems for 17 years. I thought that I would never be released from that bondage. Being in the system was a lot of hard times. I always felt that I could be dragged away at any time, and many times that's exactly what happened, but now I'm living for God and working to grow stronger in his word and living a lifestyle that would be pleasing unto him. I am a free man. Free to go where he would have me to go and do what he would have me to do. Being finally free makes me want to seek him more and learn more of what a life with God our Father will provide for me. In living for God I know that he will provide as his word says in ll. Corinthians 9:10.

Now he that ministereth seed to the sower both minister bread for your food and multiply your seed sown, and increase the fruits of your righteousness.

Elisha Aponte

To begin my testimony I must first explain a few of the things that happened to me when I was younger and some things that I got involved in. First, I came from a broken family. My father and mother separated when I was ten years old. While my father was in the home, he physically abused my mother, my brothers and me. This put a lot of mental pain in me. Even though I knew what my father was, I wanted to be with him. I held a lot of hatred towards my mother because she kept me with her.

While I was with my mother, we moved around a lot, and I was never in a stable home for very long. At one point, in one of the places where we lived, I started hanging around the wrong crowd. I started stealing, drinking and smoking cigarettes. I was only about twelve or thirteen years old at the time.

When we moved the next time, I started running away from home and ended up running the streets. My mother kidnapped me once. I was living with my father at the time. She and my brother came and got me and held me down in a car. My father had gotten remarried, and my mother was jealous of the relationship that I had with my stepmother. When my stepmother died unexpectedly, I blamed my mother for it and underwent severe emotional trauma.

I ended up hanging around with my sister again and started using drugs and running the streets with her. When I went back to my mother's house, she said she couldn't handle me anymore and let me go live with my father. While living there, I met a girl and ran away with her. We met some people who were in a cult and got involved with them. They taught us how to put curses and spells on people, and I got a tattoo.

Finally, I was locked up in a juvenile detention center for my disobedience to the law. I was there for six months and then went to a placement home for nine months. When I got out from there, I went home and started doing the things I had been previously involved in before I was locked up.

Eventually the abuse by the men in my life led me to being so depressed that I started crying out to God and praying, "Lord, I pray right now that You will send me someone I can love and who will love me." I was basically praying for a husband. Even though I was living in the world, I knew God and began to pray to Him. Not long after that, I met a boy I thought I could love, but he didn't love me. I figured out that this relationship wasn't the answer to the prayers I had lifted up to God.

Then one day I met the man who would become my husband. The moment we met we felt an instant connection with each other. The first day we talked for hours, as though we had been best friends for years. After that day, I knew God had answered my prayers and brought me a man I could spend my life with.

We did get married, but it has not been easy for us. When we started out, we had many strikes against us. First we were deep into the things of the world, doing drugs, drinking and partying. Second, our families disapproved of our relationship. Third, we had people praying bad prayers against us.

Then we became involved with this ministry, and God began to help us. Things looked good off and on for awhile, but soon we started backsliding and ended up in a jam. But God always had a hook in our mouths. We got back into the church, and when we did, God made a major move in our lives. He has healed my broken heart. I have been delivered from drugs, drinking and cigarettes. God has made Himself known to me in many ways. I've also been delivered of stubbornness, and since then God has been able to raise me up. Praise God, the last thing He has done for me so far is the best—I'm now pregnant! I know God is going to do more, and I just can't wait.

I never was taught how to be a mature woman, a wife or a mother. It is an awesome thing to see how God has helped me to mature during my pregnancy. I wouldn't let my husband go anywhere unless I was with him. What God has shown me about that is I was insecure, even though I would deny that if I was told. God had to open my eyes that I was. I also had a hard time taking care of my husband and home. When we were first married my husband would have to come home from work and then clean and cook. We used to argue about that a lot. Now in studying about women in the bible and being around godly women, I've been able to be blossom as a real woman of God. My husband has promised to be a provider for our children and thank God we have been very blessed in preparation for this child. Not only is the baby healthy and ready to be born, we also have people providing us with many things for the baby. God is always doing for people. And as we are His children, we will continue to grow strong in him and a life with him. These are some of the things that being submissive to the leadership of the ministry that God has put me under to help me to blossom in a life with him.

Gloria Johnson

I first met Pastor Dereick and Pastor Edna at church. At that time they were not yet pastors and didn't have a church of their own. Brother Dereick came to me and gave me a word from God. I had been hurt by church people in the past, so I felt that this word from God was right on time. There was so much love radiating from Brother Dereick and Sister Edna, so much so that I could not forget them

It was then that God began to draw me to both of them. The Lord told me to call Sister Edna, but I ignored His leading. The second week, God's voice became stronger to call Sister Edna. This time I simply couldn't ignore it, so I made the call. Not long after that I attended a prayer meeting in their home, and I felt the power of God in a very special way. I saw a sincerity of love and compassion in Pastors Dereick and Edna that was very real to me. Even though I was raised in a Christian home, I realize there were things lacking in my parents' Christian lives even though they were ministers. I realized I was lacking also.

The anointing in the prayer meetings at their home was very strong. Healing happened there, deliverance happened there, and bondages were broken off people's lives as well as off my own life. There was so much peace in them and their home that I didn't want to leave their presence. I felt safe.

When I would leave their presence to go home, I would ask God why they weren't pastoring a church. I knew in my heart that so many other people needed what they had to give. If Dereick and Edna went to a particular church, I would go there too. I followed them everywhere. I knew that with them I was finally home after years of searching.

As time went on I knew God wanted them to start a church. After six or seven years of teaching and ministering in the area, they finally did start a church of their own. I enjoyed seeing the presence of God come into the services. The church started at the motel and the services became more powerful.

I knew in my heart that I needed a lot of healing and deliverance in my life. God started that process when I joined their ministry. During the services, the anointing became stronger and stronger. People were being set free of all kinds of things and healings became more frequent. A year later, the church moved to another location. I saw many people come and go, but that did not stop God from moving in greater ways.

I've seen the Lord raise the pastors from one realm to the next. It blows my mind at times how God uses them in a unique way. By faith, Pastor Edna put me to work singing and taught me how to reach out to pray for people. The pastors see the potential and calling on people's lives and they push you to step out by faith into those callings, even though you may not feel worthy of the calling. But the pastors have taught me that God makes us worthy through the blood of Jesus.

I didn't realize what I could do in God until I met Pastors Dereick and Edna Smith. They display so many gifts themselves. On top of the gifts of healing, deliverance, the word of knowledge, prophecy, the word of wisdom, all the fruits of the Spirit, they have such a tremendous gift of faith, and they have confidence to operate in the gifts God has given them, for themselves and for the people. God uses the pastors to help us tap into His divine will for our lives.

Sandra Evans

I met Pastors Dereick and Edna Smith in April 2002 when I started attending their church. I brought my son to them to dedicate him to God and to ask God to heal him in the name of Jesus. When Pastors Dereick and Edna lifted my son to God, he received a miracle healing. My son was born normal. He had no problems until he reached three months of age.

Then he was diagnosed with pulmonary artery stenosis, which means one of the valves to his heart was partially blocked. Also, he would sometimes stop breathing because of the reflux coming up from his stomach. He couldn't keep any of his formula down.

My son was around five months old at the time I took him to church. He only weighed seven pounds, nine ounces. Doctors also told me that his brain was not growing. They labeled him "failure to thrive" and estimated that he would only live until he was about one year old. They said that if they were unable to correct his heart and stomach problems until he was four years old. We made trips to doctors and the specialist every week. The pediatric doctors at Hershey Medical Center refused to see him because he was too small, so we traveled back and forth to Pittsburgh. My son had a cardiology specialist, pediatric gastroenterology specialist and a pediatrician there.

After our first trip back from Pittsburgh, the pastors began to pray for my son every week. Soon every test that the doctors did on him started coming back with normal results. God was working healing in him.

Finally, his doctors labeled my son to be a normal baby who was big for his age. What a miraculous turnaround from where he had been! He only sees one pediatrician now during regular checkups.

He is now going on three years old and he runs and plays just like a normal kid. Praise God for healing my son, and thank God I had pastors who believed in God's divine healing power.

Jennifer Lane

I'm originally from Clarendon Park, Jamaica. Through a friend, I met Pastors Dereick and Edna Smith in Panama in 1983. We began a relationship in the natural, which grew into a spiritual relationship as time went on. I would go to their home and Pastor Edna would always be playing praise and worship tapes. These tapes ministered to me even though my walk with Christ was in a backslidden state. We began to have prayer three times a week, and we interceded for the presidents of our nations.

Later on, I moved from Panama to El Paso, Texas, and God sent Pastor Edna to visit me. The Lord used Pastor Edna to minister to me to move from Texas to Maryland. At the time, it seemed as though there was no way for me to move, but God made the way. They stayed in touch with me, and God used the Smiths to minister in different areas of my life.

After a while, God used Pastor Edna to speak to me about some things I was going through. I decided to come to the women's meeting at Glory to God in the Highest Church. After my first visit to the church, I felt as though I had found a home. I thank God for Pastor Dereick and Edna's faithfulness. They have taught me a lot.

Ellie Rivera

In 1983, the army sent my husband Joe to Panama and I moved there to be with him. One day, Edna Smith came knocking on my door. I knew the Lord had sent her to me. We became the best of friends with Dereick and Edna as well as with the rest of their family. God put us together and, you could say, everything else was history.

That first year in Panama, the Smiths and I were sitting at my kitchen table drinking tea and coffee. Edna gave me some cassette tapes that she had taped for me. I was very happy to have them. The Spirit of the Lord spoke to me then and God's prophetic word came forth through me for the Smiths. God said, "I have called you two to be pastors." He also told Dereick that he was going to write a book about his life in the army. After that I saw Dereick wearing a black suit and I saw the anointing of the Lord all over both of them. When the word was finished, we just praised and worshipped the Lord.

Many years passed, but we still continued to keep in touch by phone and once in a great while we would visit one another. One day the Smiths came to upstate New York to Fort Drum to see my family. At this time, the army had sent my husband away again.

We went to the PX during their visit and while there, Pastor Dereick put a black suit on layaway. The Lord spoke to my heart and told me to pay off the suit and take it out of layaway. I did all that God told me to do and told no one anything—I kept it in my heart. I wrote a letter to the pastors, and I prayed over the black suit, anointed it, and sent it to Pastor Dereick with the letter enclosed.

When Pastor Dereick received the package, he knew what was in the box even before he opened it. He told me later that he had felt the Spirit of the Lord on it. He opened the box and read the note. Then he called me and thanked God. I do thank God for Pastors Dereick and Edna Smith for they are special people in Christ and dear friends.

Lakisha Vanatta

When I first went to Glory to God in the Highest Church, I was there to hear a friend speak. There was just so much freedom in worship and so much love that I felt in that place. Part of it was the music that I heard. I was used to R&B gospel music. But when I heard the worship music there, it took me to a place in the worship realm that I had never experienced.

Later that week, God spoke to me on Wednesday and told me to move to the church I had gone to on Sunday. He also told me it was important for me to obey this so that bad things wouldn't start happening to me. I told God that He didn't have to tell me twice because I was ready to go there.

The first time Pastor Edna met me, she said to me, "Come here, sister. I don't want to shake your hand. I want to give you a hug. Powerful woman of God, you can pull down some strongholds." I looked around and I asked, "Who me?" She said, "Yes, you." She also stated to me that a person can't fly like an eagle if she hangs out with turkeys. She was seeing into my life and she said to me what no one else had ever taken the time to tell me.

I thought that I would be able to come to this ministry and do nothing. Obviously God had other plans for my life. Maturity of faith began to develop in me. God started using me in ways that I never thought I could be used. I started hearing from God like never before.

The love that Pastor Dereick and Pastor Edna walk in has compelled me to want to live right. In my time of processing, I learned how to become a better person, a better wife and a better mother. My family and I are learning how to become a real family. I have been delivered out of deep hurt. I was walked through forgiving myself, I found out that I could really be free, and I found my identity in God. Also, I learned for the first time that wearing slacks to church wasn't a sin and it didn't mean that I didn't love the Lord.

Because I never knew my father until I was twenty-seven years old, Pastor Dereick has become a spiritual father to me and also to my husband. There have been times when, as he walked past me, the love of God coming from him has been powerful enough to make me weep. I felt it just radiating right out of him. His kind hugs, which I never re-

ceived as a child, mean so much to me. All my frus-
trations, doubts, anger or other negative feeling just
melt away in his presence.

One Sunday during worship service, the anointing was very strong. My five-year-old son began to
look frantically for Pastor Edna, whom all the children call "Nanny." I asked him what was wrong and
I just knew immediately what he wanted. I walked
him over to where she was standing, and as he stood
beside her, he began to weep. The Spirit of the Lord
began to deal with his heart, and he was being delivered from things that I didn't even know were in
his heart.

Our eight-year-old son went forward for prayer
during our Thursday prayer service. The Spirit of
the Lord spoke to Pastor Dereick that if our son
would fast from Friday until Sunday a week later
(which was nine days), then God would answer his
prayers and deliver him. Jason, our son, decided that
he would fast over the dinner meal time every day.
Four days into the fast, he started crying and saying
that he was hungry. I encouraged him, telling him
that he could do it. He remembered my telling my
husband that drinking water would help, so he did
that and was just fine. Needless to say, he finished
his fast.

The following Sunday came and when he walked
into the church, the Spirit of the Lord let Pastor
Dereick know that Jason was delivered without anyone needing to lay a hand on him. He is still free

today, and he hears from God and has visions from the Lord.

I thank God for the pastors, because if they weren't in their rightful place in God these kinds of things could not take place. The power of God is evident in their lives, and it doesn't stop there. It is manifesting in our lives. Glory to God from whom all blessings flow.

Ray Vanatta

I know without a doubt what the greatest day of my life was — it was when I accepted Jesus as my Lord and Savior. My walk with God started then, but it wasn't until I met Pastors Dereick and Edna Smith that I became completely committed to and sold out for Jesus.

When I first walked through the door of Glory to God in the Highest Church, I felt the love and the peace of Jesus. I felt comfortable in church for the first time in a long time.

From that first Sunday at their church, it was only a matter of a very short time that changes began taking place within me. God demanded more of me. Pastor Dereick singled me out of all the people in the church during a service and ministered a word from the Lord to me about the hurt in my heart. Later in that service, Pastor Edna ministered to me and I felt the Holy Spirit come upon me when she placed her hand over my heart and prayed. I had never known a feeling as strong as that; I knew the Lord had touched me. I also knew there were some decisions I had to make about my life.

The next time I visited the church Pastor Edna said to me, "Don't worry anymore about if you've been called. Just realize that you've been chosen. Allow God to work in you now." Later on, I visited them in their home and I was truly blessed by them.

The pastors shed their love on me from day one. The love they offer is not just any love — it is the love of Jesus. It was experiencing that love that helped me make up my mind and purpose in my heart to live a righteous, holy, consecrated life. The pastors have helped me do this by mentoring me and keeping me accountable. They confronted me with issues in my life that most people would be afraid to confront, and I began the process of healing. There was a raging spiritual war over me, and my flesh seemed out of control. I thought I was going out of my mind. But when they began to work with me, the spirit of rejection in me was broken, the pain of having lost my daughter was broken, and I gave it all over to God with the help of the pastors.

My doctors were concerned about my sugar levels because I was diagnosed as a diabetic. I also was having extreme pain on my right side for six and a half months, and as the days went on it got worse. One Thursday night at prayer meeting, I sought the elders of the church. They anointed me with oil. Pastor Dereick laid hands on me, and the Spirit of the Lord touched me so strongly that, when I got up from being slain in the Spirit, the pain was completely gone. The stress was history. I had a doctor's appointment that following week. My doctors said that my test results were all normal. The results even showed my sugar levels to be normal. It was as though I had never been diabetic. I knew that I was healed. It has been one year since and nothing has changed. My test readings are still normal.

Pastor Dereick always has an encouraging word at the right time. He cares for and loves God's people so much. Nothing gets by him, which I know is the Christ in him. Many prophets and pastors have ministered to me before, but there was something different this time when Pastors Dereick and Edna gave me a word and prayed for me.

Since June 2002, I have learned from my pastors true love, compassion, forgiveness, patience, true salvation, holiness, peace, understanding, knowledge, wisdom and how to stand on the rock called Jesus. I learned the priorities of living a real Christian walk. Following Jesus at this church has taught me leadership skills, caring on a new level, how to be a servant, how to support a good cause, how to trust again, and how to love those who have hurt me. I've also discovered how to truly seek the Lord, how to be submissive, how to honor what God has placed in my life. I've learned gratefulness, true thankfulness, but I've especially learned how to forgive Ray, love Ray again and like Ray for who he is in the Lord. I now know my identity in Jesus. Most of all, I have learned about the love of God and have felt it from Pastor Dereick and Pastor Edna.

I am excited about my walk in God based on the changes in my life over the last year and a half. Being under true righteous leadership, those who minister from the Spirit of the Lord until the Spirit is finished has made all the difference in me. All praise, Glory and Honor to Jesus the lover of my soul.

Lisa Hoke

This is how God changed my life and how Glory to God Ministries has helped me.

I came out of a situation where God healed me on many levels. I have come to more of an understanding of God's Word and His ways. God made a way for me where there was no way. Many deliverances that only God knew on how to set me free. There were many valleys, but in my valleys the Glory to God was there for me. If it weren't for the pastors and their love and the Christ in them, I would have lost my mind. My intimacy in God has grown in such a way I could not know possible. The worship at Glory to God in the Highest, has taken me to a new level. As this year ends, 2004, I believe my intimacy with God will grow even more in the year 2005. My pastors Dereick and Edna Smith have never given up on me, and praise God for their patience. My family is Glory to God in the Highest Family Church.

Sandy Meyer

I have known Pastor Dereick and Pastor Edna Smith since I was four years old. They saw the singing gift God had placed in my life and did not take it lightly. God spoke to my mom and I to be a part of their lives and they have been teaching me and nurturing me in the things of God ever since. They have encouraged me to sing with no fear, knowing that I could do all things through Christ who gives me strength. They prayed for me, ministered to me and laid down their lives for me even in the midnight hours so that I could reach my destiny. Pastor Dereick and Pastor Edna have pushed me and encouraged me to go on with Jesus even in the hardest times of my life. It's because of them telling me that I was an overcomer by the blood of the Lamb and that I was gonna make it that I wrote the songs God has given me today. With Pastor Dereick's obedience to preach an anointed word from God I wrote an anointed song from God. Recently they just took time out of their schedule to be with me to help me cut a CD of the songs I wrote. Today, I am seventeen years old and God is doing miracles in my life because of these Pastors' obedience, prayer and support. I thank God for my spiritual parents.

CONCLUSION

Salvation is to live eternally. If you want to live eternally just say to God, "I believe Jesus died on the cross and shed His blood for me, that He arose on the third day and sits at the right hand of the Father."

For God so loved the world that He gave His only begotten Son, that whoever believes in Him should not perish, but have everlasting life. John 3:16